1978

1978

PEOPLES OF THE EARTH

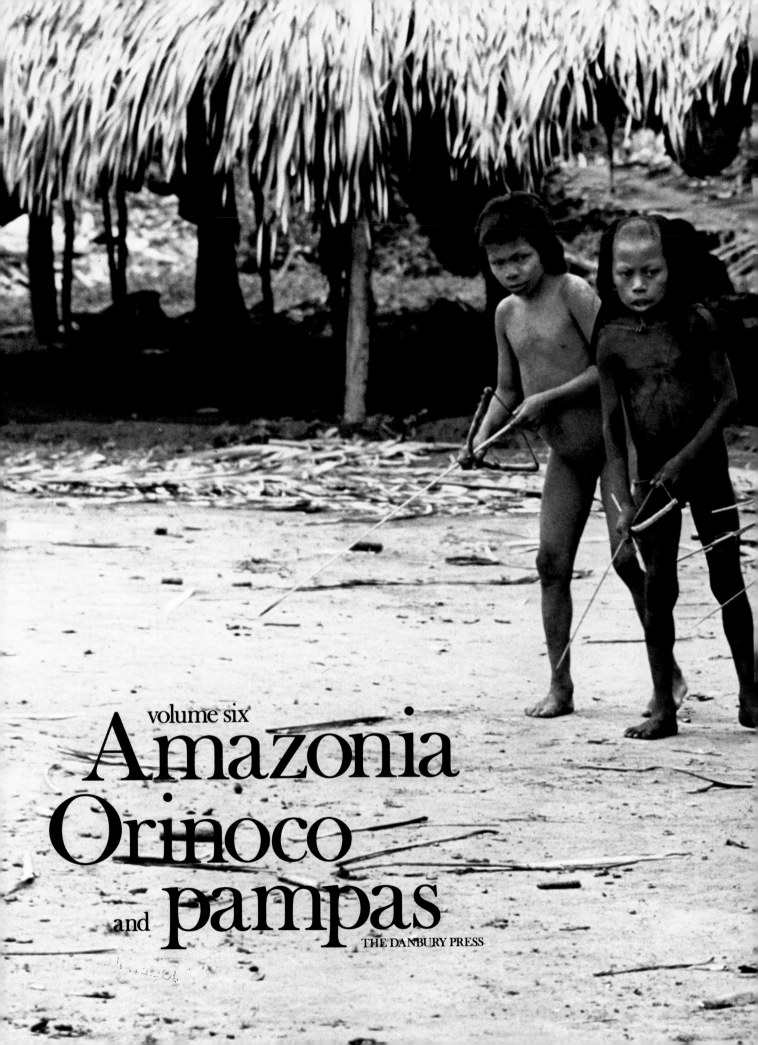

volume six
Amazonia
Orinoco
and pampas

THE DANBURY PRESS

(Preceding page) Deep in the jungle of Amazonia, young Xikrin boys with tiny bows and arrows practise hunting. One day they will have to rely for food on their stealth and skill with simple weapons.

STAFF CREDITS

Editorial Director **Tom Stacey**

Picture Director **Alexander Low**
Executive Editor **Katherine Ivens**
Art Director **Tom Deas**
Assistant Editor **Elisabeth Meakin**
Project Co-ordinator **Anne Harrison**

Specialist Picture Editor **Claire Waterson**
Picture Research **Cheryl Moyer**
Elly Beintema
Philippa Galloway
Claire Waterson
Editorial Assistants **Richard Carlisle**
Rosamund Ellis
Susan Rutherford
Xan Smiley
Design Assistants **Susan Forster**
Richard Kelly
Cartography **Ron Hayward**
Illustrations **Sandra Archibald**
Ron McTrusty

Production **Roger Multon**

The publishers gratefully acknowledge help from the following organizations:
Royal Anthropological Institute, London
Musée de l'Homme, Paris
International African Institute, London
British Museum, London
Royal Geographical Society, London
Scott Polar Research Institute, Cambridge
Royal Asiatic Society, London
Royal Central Asian Society, London
Pitt-Rivers Museum, Oxford
Horniman Museum, London
Institute of Latin American Studies, London

PHOTOGRAPHIC CREDITS
Cover – **Napoleon A. Chagnon, P. Luzuy, Bruno Barbey** (Magnum from the John Hillelson Agency), **Alexander Low.** 2,3 – **C. Andujar** (Rapho New York). 14 through 21 – **Napoleon A. Chagnon** exc.bot.lt. 16,18 and top rt. 19 – **Walter Bonatti** (Epoca). 22 through 31 – **C. Andujar** (Rapho New York) exc.top.lt. 27,29,31 – **G. Love.** 32 through 37 – **Robert Russell** and **Cornell Capa** (Magnum from the John Hillelson Agency). 38 through 40 – **P. Luzuy.** 41 – Black Star, New York, 42 through 45 – **Kenneth S. Brecher,** exc.bot. 44 – **John Moss,** 46 – Sunday Times, 47 – **Kenneth S. Brecher,** Transworld. 48,49 – **John Moss.** 50 – **H. Schultz.** 51 – **John Moss.** 52,53 – **Kenneth S. Brecher,** Sunday Times. 55 – **Kenneth S. Brecher, Adrian Cowell** (Transworld). 56 through 59 – **Thomas Hopker** (Black Star). 60 – **H. Schultz, Mike Andrews** (Camera Press), Daily Telegraph. 61 – **John Moss.** 62 – **Adrian Cowell** (Transworld), **Mike Andrews and Claude Jacoby** (both Camera Press). 63 – **Thomas Hopker** (Black Star). 64,65 – **Alexander Low.**66 – **Foto Hetzel** (Claire Waterson). 67 – **Georg Gerster** (Rapho New York). 69 – **Foto Hetzel** (Claire Waterson). 70,71 – **Bruno Barbey** (Magnum from the John Hillelson Agency). 72 through 74 – **Alexander Low.** 75 – **Armand Latovue** (Camera Press), **Foto Hetzel** (Claire Waterson). 76 through 79 – **John Bulmer.** 80,81 – **Foto Hetzel** (Claire Waterson) exc.toprt. 81 – **Bruno Barbey** (Magnum from the John Hillelson Agency). 82 – **Foto Hetzel** (Claire Waterson). 83 – **Romano Cagnoni.** 84 through 86 – **Rene Burri** (Magnum from the John Hillelson Agency). 87 – Dail Telegraph. 88,89 – **Reflejo** (Claire Waterson). 90, 91 – **Reflejo** (Claire Waterson), **Bruno Barbey** (Magnum from the John Hillelson Agency). 92,93 – **Foto Hetzel** and **Reflejo** (both Claire Waterson). 94,95 – **H. Schultz.** 96,97 – **H. Schultz, Bruno Barbey** (Magnum from the John Hillelson Agency), **Reflecjo** (Claire Waterson). 100,101 – **Foto Hetzel** and **Reflejo** (both Claire Waterson). 102,103 – **John Bulmer.** 104 – **Reflejo** (Claire Waterson). 106,107 – **John Bulmer.** 108 – **Foto Hetzel** (Claire Waterson), **Romano Cagnoni.** 110 – Daily Telegraph, **Reflejo** (Claire Waterson). 111 – **Romano Cagnoni, Reflejo** (Claire Waterson). 112 through 121 – **Foto Hetzel** (Claire Waterson). 123 through 129 – **Gordon Parks** (Peter H. Schub).

The DANBURY PRESS
a division of GROLIER ENTERPRISES INC.
Publisher
ROBERT B. CLARKE

© 1973 Europa Verlag

Printed in Italy by
Arnoldo Mondadori Editore, Verona

Contents

Supervisory Editor of the Series:
Professor Sir Edward Evans-Pritchard,
Fellow of All souls, Professor of Social Anthropology,
University of Oxford, 1946-1970,
Chevalier de la Légion d'Honneur

Volume Editor:
Dr Peter Rivière, University lecturer in Social
Anthropology, Oxford, author of *Marriage Among
the Trio: A principal of Social Organisation*, etc

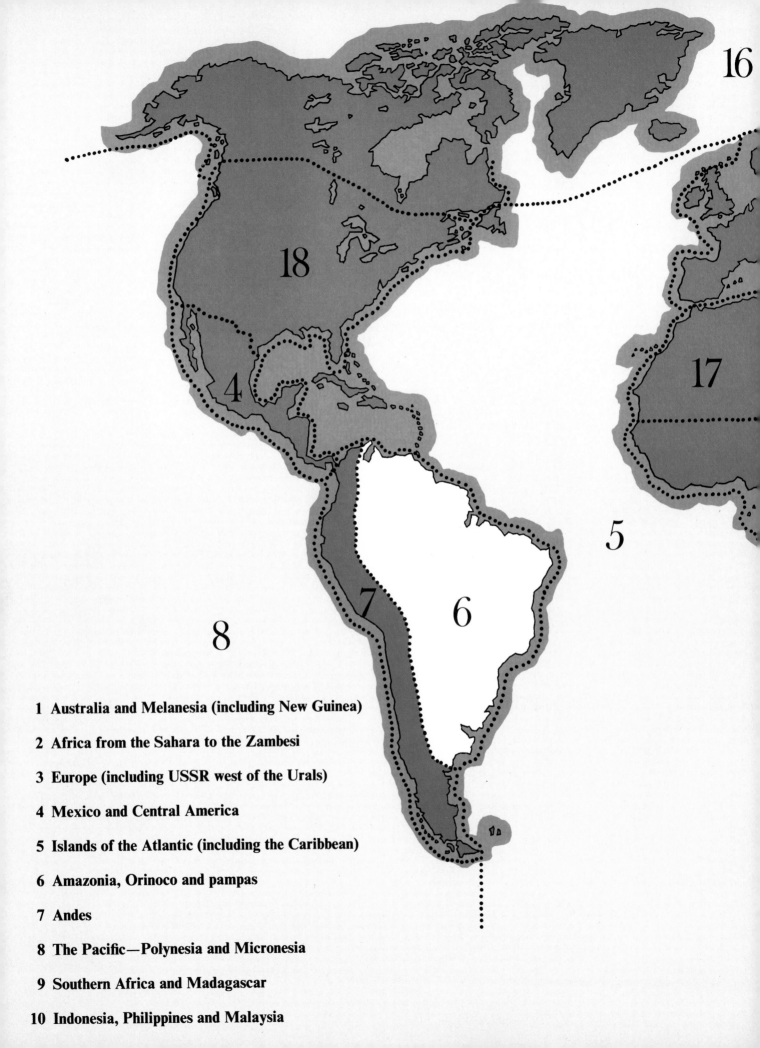

16

18

17

4

5

8

7

6

1 **Australia and Melanesia (including New Guinea)**

2 **Africa from the Sahara to the Zambesi**

3 **Europe (including USSR west of the Urals)**

4 **Mexico and Central America**

5 **Islands of the Atlantic (including the Caribbean)**

6 **Amazonia, Orinoco and pampas**

7 **Andes**

8 **The Pacific—Polynesia and Micronesia**

9 **Southern Africa and Madagascar**

10 **Indonesia, Philippines and Malaysia**

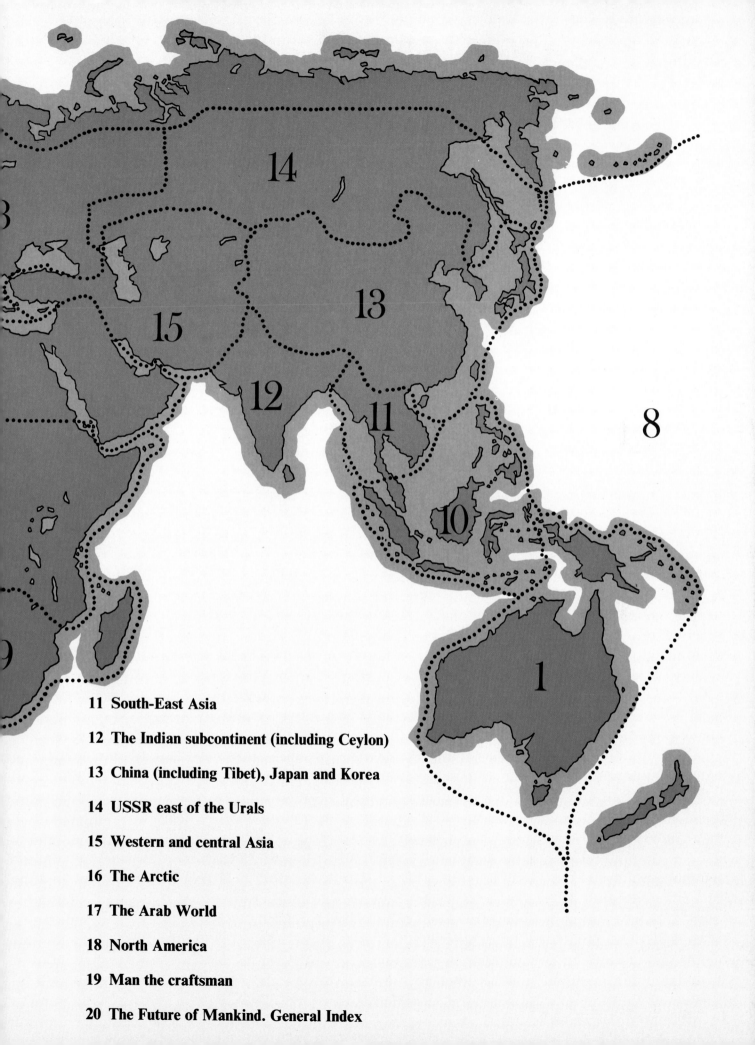

What is a tribe?

Man first banded together for the survival of the species. Almost certainly we lived in the trees in troupes, and descended from the trees in troupes. There was safety in numbers. The young could be better protected. Hunting was more effective. And simultaneously we liked being together: we developed as a social animal. But we liked being together in a defined and recognizeable group. As tasks and functions began automatically to be distributed among individual members of the group, and as the group's living and hunting area, and (later) grazing and cultivating area, came to be established, our allegiance to the group became absolute. Soon, language and myth, custom and culture, character and physique came to distinguish each of our groups from every other group. Groups became tribes, tribes nations.

In common parlance, the essential difference between a nation and a tribe is one of size and the form of cohesion. The size of any group which does, or at least can, operate as a group is determined by the range and efficiency of communication and authority. Among sophisticated, literate, technically advanced people, groups of massive size can sustain a felt allegiance and operate collectively over a vast area. This is not possible where there is no writing, and no roads or machines for swift communication. Only the personality of a mighty leader, capable of imposing a respected system of authority, can briefly weld together such a group of, say, a few million before it once again breaks up into lesser groups—which may or may not sustain a loose association with each other through the conduct of trade or war against a common enemy.

Until the spread of the written word and sophisticated communications, the size of tribes ranged from a few thousand to—at most—a few hundred thousand. Obviously, tribes in open plainlands were likely to be larger than tribes in the forest. Some tribes were, and are, limited by the extent of the terrain to which they have become adapted—like the Bakonjo of the Ruwenzori mountains, on the Congo-Uganda border, or the Anuak in the *Sudd* of the upper White Nile, or various island tribes and forest tribes. Others must range over enormous areas for economic reasons—desert tribes, for example, or Arctic tribes.

Tribal cohesion differs in form from that of the nation. As education spreads, so self-awareness enters the spirit, people tend more to see themselves as individuals, consciously aware of what binds them with their fellows, than to live as integral parts of socially self-sufficient units. Every one of us exists in our relationship with other people and other things. Our own sense of individuality thus formed varies greatly. In sophisticated society, self-conscious individualization is high—often excessively so, eating away at intuition and spontaneity and companionability. Most members of a tribal group live much more socially and environmentally submerged—in some measure, metaphorically speaking, as ants in a colony or cells in a brain. The clan or sub-group, the surrounding network of village compounds and linking paths, provide the immediate and self-sufficient society which the tribe as a whole extends and then seals.

Tribal customs and sanctions are unquestioned; life is socially secure, intuitively apprehended, and governed by forces which are never challenged. Loneliness is rare, 'orphanage' almost unknown. Men, women and often domestic animals live in close propinquity with one another and—especially in the tropics—with nature; skin is open to the elements, scented with wood smoke of the evening fires; feet become, as it were, a vegetable extension of the body—they are feet *and* shoes. Intuitive understanding is highly developed—a form of association impossible to measure and difficult to record, especially by inevitably intrusive and disturbing anthropological methods. In a group such as the Skolt Lapps, whose members are often separated for long periods because of their reindeer-herding economy, and yet whose tribal interdependence is undiminished, telepathy is so developed that conversation is sometimes hardly used when tribal members meet to reach joint decisions, after relatively long periods of separation.

Much of this is true, in some degree, in all human society, particularly in peasant society and even in working class slums or modern urban 'ghettos'. The tribe, however, tends to provide a virtually total context for the self to identify with. Its uniqueness is seemingly absolute, to any one of its members—from language to, say, cicatrization, from mythology and ancestry to the intimate sanctity of a tree, stream or rock. Tribalism is a deeply subjective affair: to many tribes the world over, the name they give themselves simply means 'people': the rest of mankind—Gentiles, barbarians, Sassenachs—are deprived of the secret of being 'people' in quite the same way. And there are tribes which have no name for themselves but use the name that others give them when presented with a rare and awkward requirement to objectivize themselves.

Authority within the tribe is also, as a rule, a defining factor. In many tribes authority takes on a broadly pyramidal structure, often repeated in a series of clans. Sometimes the pyramid is blunted, and authority stops with a cabal of elders. Sometimes it is not more than the authority of ancestors, collectively interpreted, that holds a tribe together. Single chieftainship sometimes produces remarkable men, for the men at the pinnacle may be obliged to endure a unique sense of isolation. Not infrequently it is the mildly neurotic figure who, by the very reason of his sense of difference, achieves authority within a tribe, either as a chief or, notably in Africa, as a medicine man.

Men everywhere require to make the distinction between their group and other groups. This exercise of a sense of corporate identity is bound up with the need not only for security but for self-expression. Both are as essential, in the long run, to the human species as food and shelter. The vulnerability of the tribe, or 'tribalism', in a changing world is that so much that is tribal is perishable in the face of the development of individuality and the struggle for prestige and the fascination of western technology. When western technology and the tribal world come together, tribalism is rejected not only by foreign culture that builds in steel, brick, concrete, and glass, that sings in the diatonic scale, that writes and reads stories rather than tells and listens to them, that disdains the climactic abandon of the dance; it is rejected also by a range of wholly foreign ideas—the elevation of individual personality, the spur of competition, the lust for power and material goods, the insistence on un-remitting technical progress, the obsession with ac-cumulating knowledge, the pinning down and preserva-tion of artistic creativity.

Individuality, in the sense of singleness; time, in the sense of measurement or recording of days and years; talent and spiritual insight, in the sense of a private possession—all are modified and diffused by the collec-tivity of tribal life. Distinctions have softened—dis-tinctions between life and death, between the animate and inanimate, between good and evil, between past and future. What holds the tribe together is its common experience—that is to say, itself, constantly evolving, assuming new momentary forms, skeining and re-skeining. All that comes from within the tribe, belongs to it, helps it to cohere—all of that is acceptable and good. Evil is what is strange, from outside, not comprehended. Sickness or disaster is attributed to *outside* forces. Among many tribes (specifically, today, among American Indians) strangers are by definition enemies. In every tribe, strangers are a source of fear, of unease and ob-scure disruption of realities. They are not, for example, subject to the same sanctions and precepts and are not, therefore, reachable by familiar sorcery or punishable by familiar spirits. Being beyond the range of the collective experience, they are essentially mysterious and untrust-worthy.

Someone who has been torn from a tribal environment too suddenly may be compared to a sleeper who, half-wakened, is struggling to retain a vivid dream. Psychotic breakdown frequently follows the freaks of intrusion—so common today—by sophisticated cultures upon the unsophisticated when people of tribal background (men particularly) are too peremptorily thrust into the isola-tion and competitiveness of an urban situation. Life can dramatically and suddenly seem bereft of root and meaning.

To illustrate the point I may cite an occasion when I was obliged to bring out from the depths of the highland forests of Malaya a Temiar aborigine twenty years of age, healthy, happy and alert, and take him down river to a coastal town where, for the first time in his life, he saw houses, roads, motor vehicles, bicycles, electric light, glass etc. What was the effect on him? Astonishment? Wonder? Excitement? For two days he squatted in the corner of the room I had put at his disposal, asking no questions, not even looking out of the window, showing no inquisitiveness about any aspect of his surroundings.

After two days I set off back with him up river; and three days later we were reunited with his tribal group. What was his fellows' attitude to him? Curiosity to know what he had seen and heard? Envy at his privileged adventure? Their attitude for the first few hours was one of indifference, almost of hostility. There was no barrage of questioning. Nor had he anything special that he wished to say to them. In fact, at that time he had no wish to retail anything that he had just been witnessing. Yet when a few days later others came back to the clearing after a day's successful hunting, that little community spent half the night discussing the events of the day. My companion's experience had been too re-mote from anything they or their lives consisted of. For the time being, he was restoring himself inwardly; in due course some of the more vivid impressions he had received might be spoken of.

As a group, they used to make simple wooden models of airplanes they had for some twenty years been seeing in the sky high over their forests. As a single phenomenon as inexplicable as lightning or the morning star, the air-craft had grown to be a part of the inexplicable fringe of their experience. But to encompass such a phenomenon, or the phenomena of my companion's extraordinary excursion, within their own range of logic would have involved too great a conceptual upheaval to be bearable. It would have threatened their own view of themselves, in which lay their security. Likewise my companion, one of the most intelligent of the group, was instinctively un-willing to jeopardize the collective *schema* in which his identity lay, by opening himself to all the wonders with which the little town of Kota Bahru confronted him. So he had squatted in his corner until I restored him to the community where he, Angah, made sense.

Tribal experience is, therefore, in the first place con-tained by a network of human relationships. But this network is also interwoven with place, history, animals, indeed anything that constitutes a continuing environ-ment. Nomads can carry 'environment' with them (and they do, of course, almost invariably move according to a strict rotation, pasture to pasture, well to well). But perhaps the best way to illustrate a collective factor in tribal existence is to observe the pattern of life on and around the earth compound of a tropical village forty or fifty feet across, where the intrusion of western life is still unmarked.

Ebumpomboli is on a ridge of the Ruwenzori foothills 9

in Uganda overlooking the Ituri Forest of Zaïre (Congo). The Bakonjo villagers have summoned their fellow tribesmen from neighboring ridges for a celebration in music, dancing and beer of the peaceful settlement of a long drawn-out quarrel with their neighbors, the Bamba, who live beneath them on the mountains. Messengers from Ebumpomboli had gone out to summon the famous *eluma* team from settlements across all the Bakonjo ridges on the west side of Ruwenzori. In a day or two, the *eluma* team would be assembled to blow their bearded flutes and perform their exceptional dance. But there is no haste.

Preparation for the dance mounts gradually. The false nights of fog merge with the dark evenings when men play their instruments, and talk, and gaze into the fire. There is continuity of sound. The cock crows in the foggy dawn. Even in the morning one is reminded of the young man who had been in his hut doorway late into some previous darkness with his two-stringed fiddle, made of a stick and calabash and fiber 'string' that buzzes like a three-noted insect droning against its own varying rhythm—for the small sound is still audible from one of the huts. The villagers have become surrounded by music, and other rhythms, even singing, being drawn in by the music as water by earth.

The armlet weaver is working quickly, like someone crocheting, outside the hut's entrance, his fingers calloused by the fiber he works. He has the face of a craftsman and a voice that is patient, especially when explaining his craft to his apprentices. As in all languages, meaning exists to some extent in the sound of the sentences—but here more so, since in spoken Bantu the individual association of each word with the whole sentence, and the tendency to rhyme sentences alliteratively, are greater than with languages that have been long dominated by their written form. The distinction between simile and metaphor on the one hand, and that which is being objectivized by language on the other, is less sharp than the westernized are accustomed to. The constant use of metaphor reinforces the true unity of everything.

Out there on the compound and children have a drum; and for them the drum, that has been part of a tree, might contain a spirit—one and manifold. Usually it is a big drum out there. It is the boys that drum; a small boy of two or three drums it with a couple of sticks and rattles the mountainside for a few seconds. Then the big boys come and beat it regularly for several minutes, two or three of them at once. Then the men get on it. When three flute players are also out there on the compound, one on a stool, one on a log, women assemble on the edge like a big weed after a gale across water; but the children are already bobbing and dancing there. The sun reaches under the curved entrance shadow of the hut of the armlet weaver where his wife squats making a fire, and a meal

in a clay pot between three stones. The weaver works on, looping, threading, rethreading, bracing the armlet circle against a forked stick gripped in prehensile feet. Once, they will have all remembered, armlets from the yellow fiber of the single *olutegha* tree—whose seed was brought by their ancestor from a distant land where their forefathers lived—were currency. Now goats are currency.

Everywhere among tribal people there are drums. The drum is the summoner, the unifier, the warner. It draws to any compound those that belong there; to the outsider it is an expression of jealously protected intimacy. The drummer is constantly improvising. There is no planned order, no rising pitch, no framed related harmonies, no lines of melody or counter-melody, but endlessly varying, instantly superseded, rhythmic patters. The drummer seeks to achieve nothing; his drumming is elusive, subjective, summoned out of the void. The drummer's hands work like the hands of a potter, but in clay that is always soft and wet and never produces a hard durable figure.

Women in their bangles and neck rings, now returning early from the cultivation strips with babies tied in goatskins on their backs, or, burdened with great baskets, climbing up from the lower hills have their approach observed by the others aurally, by the clink of their metal ornaments. The markedly veined smith works in the fantastically cobwebbed hut at the end of the compound to ring young girls with metal for life. Everyone on the compound can see just the back of the smith's son working the big goat-skin bellows, until the mother of the little boy who first beat on the drum comes and stands between, feeding from her breast that same three-year-old, still unweaned.

The compound is now choking with children; and some of the men who are to play the *eluma* flutes evict, with their feet, the brown sheep in whose hard skin jiggers have burrowed to lay their eggs. Slowly the celebration is gathering attention. The married women have no role of their own to play here; but the old ones watch through the hut walls of bamboo stem leaves, scraping the millet porridge bowls. Others watch from the path coming in from three directions; others from cultivated patches, planting millet, bending horizontal. One woman lying sick in her hut, her child dead within her, watches the sound.

Men and women come and go. Men stand in groups out in the sun, having crossed from other ridges for the dance. Sometimes the old women will get up from behind the fires in the huts and, their old dry goat skins crackling, pass beside the compound to fetch water from the stream a short descent beyond the smithy's hut. One of them close by is picking out a new goat skin, and the pricks make a popping sound audible through the music. Like the men and women, sheep and goats are coming and going. Some sit in groups, brown and white in the sun. There are ten great clay jars of banana beer.

Each of the players has a tiny single-noted reed pipe: together the reeds run up a chromatic octave and overtop it a tone or two, and the players revolve blowing, eleven of them, working intensely, yet their odor inoffensive because it is not individual. Each reed they blow, a presage of eternity cut from the limitless lowland forest by pygmies who perform such things for all neighboring tribes along the forest perimeters, is sheathed with brown woven grass stained alternately dark to chequer it, and enclosed by the right hand from which the blocked reed tip emerges masked mysteriously by a beard of colobus monkey fur. The sound is like a choir of archaic record-ers in roughly disciplined disharmony, *cantores* blowing while *decani* breathe in—an irreligious syncopation mesmerizing by sound and movement, by circling in intimate, primitive dance round drums, involving sym-bols of sexual display, flirtatious advance and the sudden retreat, but nothing consciously calculated. The sun is at its zenith and buries shadows.

The present sound has now stirred other people watching in the huts. Heavy breasted young mothers come slowly out like rock fish and boys and babies run into the center to imitate, where they are immediately accepted. Chickens enter into empty huts to peck at fire edges. Comedians among the dancers emerge posturing from the throng to make exaggerated turns; but most are serious, together urging from their circling bodies utmost controlled expression in series of hops and shakings of every muscle and sudden twists of loins and turning flicks of hindquarters in bark cloth. They hold their hands forward, their arms half bent, and eyes are fixed in con-centration. The threaded monkey teeth which rattle on the woman when she carries her child and when she thumps cassava in her mortar, and when she beats water into clay on her stone built pots, now rattle dancing. The many-reeded music sounds like a single old fashioned concertina of enormous force and impulsively jerked open and squeezed, fingers shifting blindly on the keys.

Yet there are symptoms of design, and even at intervals the circle of rapidly strutting male bodies bends down in-wards towards the drum, the *eluma* players also, but still blowing—then all right themselves. This movement is one of obeisance towards those spirits present: the dancers are receiving life. At the perimeter the women, aware of what the men are receiving, never actually look directly, knowing such physical power as too precious to be consciously hoarded or to be expended in social sexuality (for the symbols of the dance are self-contained), but that it would be kept in bond between man and his spirits until the momentary secret collision of the two perpetual elements of sexuality—the unconscious union of maleness and femaleness that rests in the tribe. And by now the white-headed chief, a powerful purveyor of ancestral forces, has himself joined the shaking, jerking, angled limbs that compose the rotating human reed

organ round the three thrashing drums.

As it subsides, fog descends, at first wispily. Out on the compound there is still one drum going, the biggest one, the boys too small for shepherding beating it. Another drum, with a flute, in a hut below the compound, con-tinues; and in a distant compound, just within earshot, there is yet another drum, infected by the celebration, and still excited. The fog remains until darkness. Later, two flutes begin again, like the songs of birds assembled by spirits, and with the darkness the huts fill with men—more this night than usual.

One of the lute players, a full faced young man, son of the chief, with a monkey skin clinging round his neck and down his back, enters his father's hut during a silence and puts the bamboo barrier behind him against the wind. The white-headed chief himself, commanding everyone in his ordained relationship to them, sits leaning on his stool against the wall over the fire, feet apart and elbows on his closed knees, his old smoked eyes searching into the fire. His chieftainship is his pre-occupation, as it must be. His old men lean towards him, nearest the fire, their eyes also joining in the fire, passing the long petiole pipe from mouth to mouth, sharing it like thought.

11

Peoples of lowland South America

The basins of three huge river systems, the Amazon, Orinoco and Paraguay-Parana, occupy all but a fraction of lowland South America. The network of waterways made by these rivers lends a peculiar unity to the region, since except for a short portage it is possible to travel by boat from one end of the area to the other. A traveler entering the Orinoco delta can make his way upstream to where the natural channel, known as the Cassiquiare Canal, connects with the Amazonian system. Then he goes down river to take one of the Amazon's south bank tributaries leading to the Mato Grosso. Here, in central Brazil, there is only a short overland haul to the waters of the Paraguay-Parana basin which will bear our traveler to the estuary of the River Plate. If he then turns northward along the coast and pursues his journey to the mouth of the Amazon, he will have sampled at first hand nearly a complete cross-section of the peoples portrayed in this volume.

In such a journey he would experience some major contrasts of the area; between tropical jungle and temperate grassland; coast and interior; 20th century cities and Amerindian huts; rich and poor; the old world and the new world. This journey would also be an interesting historical experience, for the development of the entire area has followed the distribution of its navigable rivers and coastal waters. In spite of modern technology, especially the aeroplane and the motor vehicle, three quarters of Brazil's population live within one hundred miles of the coast. And early accounts indicate that there were large Indian populations along the coasts and main rivers when the Europeans first arrived – although the difficulties involved in taking any comprehensive archaeological survey make it impossible to be absolutely sure.

At certain times and in certain places the Amerindians were strong enough to repulse the new arrivals for a short time, but most of the original inhabitants vanished early on. Some were killed fighting; others died in massacres or in slavery; the majority perished victims of new diseases to which they had no resistance; and the lucky ones fled into the remoter regions. Our traveler could witness much of this and more for it is still possible to observe a historical process over four centuries old – the advance of a frontier.

The story of European entry into the eastern lowland area of South America contrasts with the story of entry into the western, highland region. In the west there was no interference from other would-be colonial powers, and the Spaniards found and captured, virtually at a single stroke, a complete empire. And to the east, the Spaniards early laid claim to what are now Venezuela, Argentina, Paraguay and Uruguay. But with the vast area that was to be Brazil the situation was rather different. Under the Treaty of Tordesillas (1494) the Spanish and Portuguese crowns had agreed to divide the world: the Spaniards would take the west and the Portuguese the east. Ignorant of geography, the signatories accepted a demarcating line which gave eastern Brazil to Portugal. Portugal, was then, as ever, short of manpower and preoccupied with her East Indian possessions; and so it was not until the second quarter of the 16th century that she was to pay any real attention to South America. By then the Portuguese had to contend with the French who were energetic on the coast during that century, the English who had settlements on the lower reaches of the Amazon until well into the 17th century, and the Dutch who controlled large areas of the coast until 1654.

In eastern South America, unlike western South America, all these European powers had the disadvantage to contend with that in this region were no united Indian empires there for the taking. Each tribe, often each village, was an autonomous political unit, and each had to be pacified, subjugated or treated with separately. The frontier advanced unevenly as deep inroads were made along the larger waterways while the remoter headwaters and interfluvial divides were left untouched. Today a similar form of ribbon development is occurring along the new roads that are being constructed in the region. It is this unevenness in the frontier's progress which allows the modern traveler – and the reader of this volume – to witness all stages of this historical process.

This area contains more unknown territory than exists elsewhere in the world. There are, for example, people like the Kreen-Akrore who have never been seen by a white man. Beneath the thick canopy of the tropical forest there are almost certainly tribes uncontacted and even unheard of. The forest remains a fastness for small groups which have chosen to have nothing to do with strange intruders. A combination of remoteness and fierceness has allowed the Jivaro and the Yanomamo to retain their tribal vigor more or less intact. Indeed the Yanomamo, during what has been for other tribes a time of rapidly declining population, have managed to reverse this trend, and have expanded both demographically and territorially. The Xikrin, and linguistically related tribes such as the Shavante, have held up the advance of the Brazilian frontier for many years during this century. But fierce or not these tribes tend finally to succumb. Thus the various tribes who inhabit the headwaters of the Xingu River and its environs are almost certainly the descendants of those who retreated there many generations ago in the face of the advancing frontier. Today, there is nowhere left for them to go, and decimated by disease and deprived of much of their land they await the fate of their ancestors.

Their future is anticipated in the condition of the Guarani, a once numerous people who occupied a vast area of the Paraguay-Parana basin. Victims of slave raiders and pawns in a power struggle between church and state, their survivors are now reduced to the lower levels of Paraguyan society, although they have partly managed to retain their own language. The final stage in this process of disintegration can possibly best be seen within the Amazon region where isolated, detribalized Indians, ashamed to speak their own language even if they know any of it, are reduced to speaking rustic Spanish and Portuguese.

This is the lowest limit of Indian life. At this stage the Indian is indistinguishable from the local peasant. In Brazil the same term, *caboclo*, is applied indiscriminately to both. The *caboclo* is a subsistence cultivator who uses crude agricultural methods to grow a limited range of crops, and makes little effort to exploit his environment further save for occasional charcoal burning, rubber tapping or Brazil nut collecting, to earn the small amounts of cash he needs. His life is of abject squalor and his expectations no wider than the clearing in which he lives. His standard of living is far below that of the tribal Indian whom he invariably despises as an animal.

This low standard of living is restricted to neither the forest area nor to one ethnic group. The *jangada* fisher-men on the coast of north-east Brazil gain only a bare subsistence from the sea, while inland the inhabitants live even closer to the margins of existence. In this area cattle ranching has traditionally been important but the industry has never been developed to the high level achieved on the grasslands of southern Brazil, Uruguay and Argentina. It is an area of uncertain rainfall and although extensive irrigation schemes in the São Francisco river valley have done something to alleviate the situation droughts at frequent intervals drive a large proportion of the rural population into the cities to swell the rapidly growing numbers of urban poor.

In the cities of lowland South America there is virtually no cheap housing for people who do the menial tasks for the better-off city dwellers. Shanty towns, or favelas as they are called in Brazil, spring up around old and new cities alike wherever land is available. Brasilia, for example, was quickly ringed by them, often only a few minutes' walk from the richest quarters of the city.

Although the population of these shanty towns is, as elsewhere, an amalgam of European, Amerindian and African stock it is perhaps the people of African origin who, through literature and films, have become popularly associated with the favelas. There is some truth behind this popular image, for these favelas reach their greatest extension in the Brazilian cities from São Paulo north-wards, where there are more people of African descent.

This African population is descended from the four million or so slaves who were transported across the Atlantic into South America as cheap manpower for the sugar plantations. Metropolitan Portugal could never have provided labor on this scale and anyhow the aristo-cratic pretensions of the immigrants did not dispose them towards manual labor. Not only did the colonists quickly discover that the Amerindians were of inferior quality as slaves and limited in numbers, but the church and state were also forever placing difficulties in the way of enslaving them. The large African element in the population has endowed the culture of Brazil with a particular quality. One of the most striking aspects of this so-called Afro-Brazilian culture are the religious cults, such as macumba, which are syncretisms of African and Christian beliefs. But it would seem also that today it is from this lower and mainly African class that Carnaval, the great pre-Lenten feast, derives its spontaneity, a quality which the upper and middle class celebration of the feast seems to lack.

It has been argued that Brazil has no middle class – but that depends on which Brazil one talks about. There is Brazil from São Paulo northwards where both African and Amerindian elements are most pronounced and where Portuguese is the most common European ancestry. Here the great sugar plantations arose, and the idea of the Brazilian patriarchal family centered on the plantation developed. But southward from São Paulo through Uruguay into Argentina there can be no doubt about the existence of a middle class.

Here in the south the atmosphere is far more European: Italian, Scandinavian and German. So strongly have some communities retained their nationality of origin that it is possible to arrive in a small town and feel at once that one has been transported several thousand miles to Europe. It has not only been from Europe that the immigrants have come: some of the most influential recent arrivals in Brazil have been Japanese. Many Japanese have settled in large commercial centers, but they also work plots of land in the interior: wherever they are, their industriousness has led them to success.

Until now the peoples of lowland South America have been primary producers for the more highly developed industrial nations of North America and Europe. Sugar has come from north-east Brazil, rubber from the Amazon basin, coffee from the State of São Paulo, beef from the pampas of Argentina and Uruguay, and oil from Venezuela. There are now signs of a swing away from their role as primary producers and, led by Brazil, the countries of this area appear to be on the verge of their own industrial revolution. Whatever its effects it is unlikely that the fundamental features of peoples observed by our traveler will change much in the next decades. The process of frontier development still has some way to run and the orientation of the bulk of the population remains focussed on the cities of the coastal belt.

Yanomamo
Brazil and Venezuela

Yanomamo life revolves round fighting. Chest-pounding or head-bashing duels can escalate into free-for-alls with clubs and axes.

The Yanomamo are an exceptionally fierce, warlike people. They present a rare opportunity for modern urban man, conscious that the civilizations of the 20th century have never come to terms with turbulent and often pointless violence within and between his own communities, to study violence 'in the raw'. There are less than 15,000 Yanomamo Indians. They live in Venezuela and Brazil in widely scattered villages, seldom larger than 200 inhabitants, with little contact and conflict with the outside world. Their agriculture is prosperous; game is prolific; and yet hostilities between villages are not only savage and murderous, they are also almost unceasing. If a village can find no evidence of an attack by another then it may find a less tangible reason for aggression: it may claim that sickness and disease among its members is the result of sorcery by the other village. Their wars and duels are as much a part of their lives, as struggle and competition are of western society.

The Yanomamo Indians sustain their hostilities by 15

Yanomamo Brazil and Venezuela

The hallucinogenic drug *ebene* is cultivated in all Yanomamo villages. Here a man blows it through a reed tube into his friend's nostrils.

Two men in a hallucinatory stupor induced by *ebene* believe their intoxication brings them into contact with the *hekura* spirits.

cultivating food-crops using the slash-and-burn technique: clearing a small patch of the tropical forest, burning it, then planting the plot with root-cuttings or seeds – their main crops are plantains (bananas), cassava, sweet potatoes and yams which successfully bear fruit with little extra care. Two or three hours' work a day is sufficient to feed an entire village well. They also eat caterpillars, termites and fish, caught from streams poisoned with *barbasco*. They grow cotton, tobacco, arrowcane and plants which yield hallucinogenic drugs, and they hunt birds, monkeys, tapirs and wild pigs.

The Yanomamo could grow more food in their fertile forest if they wanted to, but it would be wasted. They only produce a surplus for gifts to other villages, tokens of friendship when one village wants to make an alliance with another. And so their wars and hostilities cannot be explained away by saying they are a natural means of controlling a population the forest could not support. The forest can support the Yanomamo with no difficulty whatsoever.

Yanomamo villages are independent political entities and constantly liable to attack by any one of their numerous neighbors – intensity of warfare will vary from place to place and time to time but the circumstances in which an attack will be made are well defined and understood by all. As no village overlooks the possibility that its neighbors will someday turn on them and abduct their women, each makes demonstrations of its strength.

And each group knows that its flaunted independence is limited, for sooner or later when, as is inevitable, it is attacked by a larger village it will have to call on a neighbor that it needs (but cannot trust) to come to its aid. It is a strained political situation in which the strong always dominate the weak, and in which every village must maintain a show of strength and ferocity to inspire fear and respect in its neighbors, who might be allies or might be foes.

Each village goes in for violent duelling. Sometimes duelling is controlled and disciplined. Chest-pounding or side-slapping duels, either between two factions of the same village or between two separate villages, are the simplest and least serious expressions of ferocity and demonstrate the strength of the participant. But at other times it is unrestrained and escalates into outright warfare. Stealing food, committing adultery or insulting somebody's courage are all good excuses for a duel which can end up as a serious fight. One man will stand with his arms at his side, his head back and his chest prominently exposed. His assailant winds up with all his force, and delivers a mighty blow to the man's chest, often knocking him down. The recipient of the blow or blows then has his turn to hit the assailant and may hit him as many times as he himself was struck. Once a fight starts, every adult male in the village becomes involved, each taking several turns until either the grievance is settled or the fight escalates to clubs. There are other variations of the

chest-pounding duel; sometimes the opponents strike each other on the side, between the ribs and the hip, or use the blunt side of an axe or the flat of a machete blade. Deaths are not uncommon.

Fights with clubs – sharpened, springy poles 8–10 feet long – are also prearranged and restrained by rules and regulations, but they are more violent. A man will jab his club into the ground and lean against it with his head exposed for his opponent to strike. Then the opponent wallops him on the head with a staggering blow, tearing the scalp and hair away with the impact. Now it is the opponent's turn to expose his head for the first man to reciprocate the blow. It is a measure of the Yanomamo ferocity that the scalps of most brave fighters are crisscrossed with dozens of deep, ugly scars. When, as often happens, the onlookers are divided in their support of the protagonists, the first blow precipitates a free-for-all, as the men on one side swing wildly at the line of their opponents. The supporters' allegiance may be based on kinship or, more rarely, on sympathy for the justness of one of the protagonist's claims.

If an issue is so serious or the fighting so desperate that deaths are likely to result, the headman or headmen stand aside with bows and arrows, threatening to kill anyone who violates the rules and tries to esclate the fighting to a more serious level. In one such fight, the headman took another man's club away from him after he had jabbed his opponent with the sharpened end. Then the headman ran the other through with the club and left him to die in the village clearing. The fight ended.

Warfare, different from the formal duels, involves raids on enemy villages with intent to kill, and then retreating before the enemy discovers the death.

To reach their enemy, raiders may have to travel for more than a week through the tropical rain-forests. They approach the village at dawn, surround it and wait for a hapless man to wander out alone. They shoot him and retreat hastily, often running all day and night to flee from their possible pursuers. These surprise attacks, although they seldom result in many casualties, are so frequent that in one area one out of every four males who reaches adulthood is expected to die at the hands of raiders. Primitive warfare is often described as ceremonial or ineffective. With this kind of result Yanomamo warfare could hardly be dismissed as ceremonial.

But the most savage form of Yanomamo violence is the *nomohori*, or trick. A group with a particularly strong hatred for its enemies will solicit the aid of a third village that is on relatively friendly terms with the intended victims. The third village arranges a feast for the unsuspecting victims, and while they are lying defenseless in their hammocks, the treacherous hosts fall upon them with sharpened staves, axes and arrows. Those who survive the massacre inside are ambushed by the instigators of the treachery, who lie in wait outside. Many women are taken captive during these treacherous feasts and **17**

Climbing a *rasha* tree to collect the palm fruit, this man avoids the sharp spines by using two pairs of crossed poles strapped to the trunk.

The dammed stream has been poisoned with *barbasco* by the men. Now the stupefied fish are collected in baskets by the women.

The building of houses requires much co-operation. Poles must be cut and set; vines and leaves gathered for thatching into the roof

shared by the two victorious groups.

Daily life in a village that is beleaguered by frequent raids is nothing short of frenzied and hectic. The adults are constantly agitated and bickering. Women are afraid to leave the village to collect firewood, gather plantains or fetch water; the men are touchy and constantly on the alert. Any strange noise outside the village, any dog bark or sudden shout precipitates general panic as the men jump up, grab their weapons and stand ready with drawn bows, trembling all over. False alarms are frequent. Three or four days in such a village is enough to reduce even the most sober outsider to a nervous wreck.

In these villages, under the constant threat of enemy raids, arguments and squabbles between villagers are also frequent; the larger the village, the more likely it is that any small argument will develop into a club-fight. The dispute may arise over a caustic comment and a man will set upon its author with a hail of insults and blows from a machete, club or axe. A large village will have dozens of smouldering grievances, any of which is liable to explode with the slightest provocation. The village's political organization is incapable of restraining or dealing with groups of much more than 150 people.

By the time a village reaches a population of 100 or so people, there are so many disputes, so much factionalism that village life can be totally disrupted. The villages can maintain this size only if the headmen are particularly forceful and authoritative, and if villagers are more strongly linked by kinship than they are divided by disputes. In the end only the pressure or threat of war prevents the Yanomamo village from disintegrating. The threat of war also stimulates the villages to continue growing as small villages of 50 people are at a disadvantage against neighboring villages of 100 or more people. As villages reach 150 or 200 people in total size, inter-village fighting becomes a constant problem. When villages fragment (normally long before their population reaches 200) the newly-formed independent villages often separate from each other on hostile terms, one of them migrating far away to initiate raids against the old

Every Yanomamo family has to cultivate its own tobacco. Chewed by men, women and children, it is the crop most commonly stolen.

19

Yanomamo Brazil and Venezuela

The village is composed of a
ring of houses; after 2 years
it is burnt down because
of cockroaches, spiders and
scorpions in the hut-roofs.

With bows and arrows, men
from the village prepare to
leave on a raid; they sing
'I am meat-hungry, like the
carrion eating buzzard!'

A man dips his arrow point in *curare* poison; it will be used to kill monkeys. For a raid on an enemy, unpoisoned arrows are – sportingly – used

group. Blood relatives then become fierce enemies.

Villages 'A' and 'B' might be bitter enemies in one decade, but friends during the next. Because of the constantly shifting warfare, friendships and animosities rapidly develop out of each other. In the last stages of an alliance, Group A might invite Group B to a feast and there fall upon them with savage treachery.

The simplest form of alliance is a trade arrangement between two villages. By their trade the villagers can forge a relationship in which each group can turn to the other in time of duress, although the villagers would strenuously deny it, and concentrate their attention on the trading commodities – dogs, bows, arrows, spun cotton yarn, hammocks, baskets, clay pots and hallucinogenic drugs.

As trade builds up the two groups begin visiting and holding feasts for each other. They drink the cremated remains of each others' dead in solemn cannibalistic ceremonies. They offer marriageable women to one another and give refuge when raiding becomes particularly intense. But these alliances are always tenuous and rarely last many years. Chest-pounding duels and club-fights begin to punctuate the friendship. Trust begins to flounder as each group resents the demands of the other. Sooner or later one of the groups demands more women than the other is willing to give in return, and the stronger group may forcibly take the women from the weaker group. They cultivate alliances with other villages. The allies drift further and further apart until often they become bitter enemies.

Most deaths, save for those resulting from warfare, are considered to be the result of malevolent actions caused by shamans in enemy villages. Infant mortality and death from disease are so common that villages constantly accuse each other of harmful sorcery. Each day, therefore, the men of the village take *ebene*, an hallucinogenic snuff powder made from various wild and cultivated plant products, and call upon the *hekura* spirits to destroy the souls of their enemies and cause them to waste away and die.

The shamans assemble, blow quantities of the hallucinogenic *ebene* into each other's nostrils, and invoke their *hekura* either to attack enemies or prevent the enemy's *hekura* from attacking them. Initially sniffing the drug is painful. It causes retching and vomiting and produce terrible headaches afterwards. But there is a perpetual need to defend oneself and one's group from the depredations of the enemy shamans and so the drugs must be taken daily to keep in contact with the spirits. Though warfare may wane, war between spirits never relinquishes its hold on the Yanomamo. A death in another village is cause for celebration.

Shamans publicly take credit for causing the death. And the word of this reaches the other village – who increase their magic and even begin raids. The animosities are soon renewed.

21

At a feast given by one village for its allies in another, the Yanomamo eat *date*, a thick soup made from ripened plantains.

Xikrin
Brazil

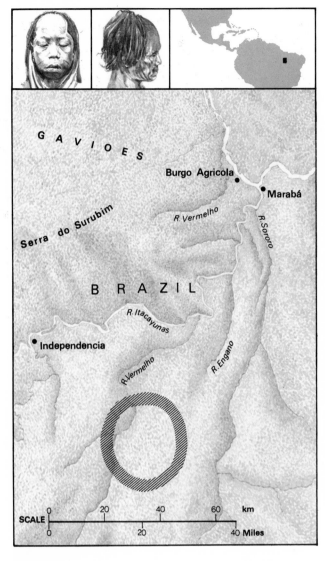

The Xikrin are a warlike people. Until recently these Cayapo people have fought off the aggression and intrusion from Brazilians and other Indians alike; both with extraordinary success. There is nothing about the country in which they live that encourages such ferocity. The Xikrin inhabit the most northerly part of the Cayapo lands, closest to the Amazon river where they are presented with no desperate struggle for existence, no need for fortitude or aggression. Xikrin country, the richest and lushest of all Cayapo country is, however, worth defending.

The flat lands of the Cayapo are 1,000 feet above sea-level. In places they are covered with semi-deciduous rainforest, elsewhere there is grassy savanna, parklands with dry scrub trees. Everywhere the land is broken up by low ridges and slopes which reach up into the Brazilian Central Plateau. By the Amazon river the rainforest

23

Xikrin paint their babies
with dark blue paint. It gives
them pleasure and makes
them sleep. Geometrical
designs are made by stiletto.

Xikrin warriors meet at dusk
to discuss the day's events
and perhaps to plan warfare
or hunting techniques
for the following day.

is infinitely richer in plant and animal life than either the interior of the Amazon rainforests or the grassy savannas further south and east. Of both forest and savanna the semi-nomadic Xikrin take easy advantage.

From October to early June, the rainy season, the Xikrin live in their villages, cultivating sweet potatoes and maize on communally owned gardens in forest clearings, where the effect of cutting down trees, drying and burning the wood has particularly enriched the soil. They also grow yams and sweet manioc. They hunt turtles, gather Brazil nuts, and fish, using both hooks and poison, with enough success to give plenty of variety to their diet. So abundant are the forests during the rainy season that a small group of Xikrin women will, in just three hours' hunting, bring home 27 large delectable turtles; in a full year, the Xikrin will consume as many as 2,000 turtles. Village life for the ferocious Xikrin tends to be gentle and leisurely. There is always time to indulge in the art, beloved to all Cayapo, of body-painting.

In the dry season between June and September, entire family groups – all but the old and sick who remain in the villages in the care of relatives – uproot themselves to roam the forest and grassland, hunting and searching for futher provender. More turtles are collected, more nuts and now wild fruits, hearts of palm, honey and many

(Left) Xikrin call themselves
people of the watery place'.
The most northerly of the,
Cayapo tribal group, they live
close to the Amazon.

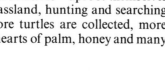

This still suckling child
had his ears pierced when
he was only weeks old and
filled with wooden plugs,
brightly dyed with paste.

other delicacies too. They balance this luxury diet, (and keep an eye on the sick and old at home) by periodically dispatching the youths of the family back to the village for cultivated foods. Occasionally a family will make an overnight stop in their home village as they move from one forest area to another.

It is an enviably easy life in which food is there for the picking. But it is likely that the Xikrin fought as hard to secure it as they have fought recently to defend it.

Little is known either of their origins or their history. Xikrin (pronounced 'Tcheekreen') is how they describe themselves to the Brazilians in their locality, who also sometimes call them the Djore, or 'sweet potato people'. Among themselves, however, the Xikrin call themselves Mebengokre – by which they clearly associate themselves with the land which yields them so much food. Mebengokre means 'people of the watery places'.

According to the Xikrin's own account of their origins, they once lived with their cousins the Gorotire-Cayapo in the Rio Fresco region. Then, four or five generations ago, they had a fight with the Gorotire-Cayapo over a cornfield and moved off in search of new lands. By 1900 the Xikrin had burst out of the territories traditionally occupied by the Cayapo and overwhelmed the lands of a number of tribes some eight miles north-east in the Caitete-Ita-Caiunas river area. This is confirmed by an encounter that the foremost Xikrin ethnologist, Protasio Frikel, had in 1962 with an old Brazilian, who, in 1903, made peaceful contact with the Xikrin, just after they had moved in to the Caitete region. Soon after the Xikrin arrived, the old man told Frikel, hostilities flared up, not between the Xikrin and the Indians of the region, but between the Xikrin and other invaders of the area. These were the Brazilian rubber tappers, followed by Brazil nut gatherers and gold panners. The Xikrin vociferously resisted these intruders too. They followed attack with counter-attack and, sometimes, massacre with massacre. Only in 1954 were the Xikrin finally 'pacified' and settled by the Indian Protection Service in the same Caitete territory they secured in 1900.

Young Xikrin warriors are raised by their mothers with the most loving care. There is nothing of ferocity in their early upbringing: Xikrin families live all together in a hierarchy of female authority – grandmother, daughters, grand-daughters, husbands, sons, brothers— in the family hut. This stands with twelve other similar huts, around an oval or circular central plaza in which the people of the village gather for meetings and ceremonies. At one end of the oval is the chief's house; at the other the men's house. The women of the village have their own area by the village oven behind the chief's house. The family can look out onto the plaza from inside the hut, which has no windows, but on the plaza side, has no wall, only a thick curtain of palm straw which reaches down from the roof to the ground. Through this, families can watch everything that is going on outside without

themselves being seen. The hut is built of 28 poles and rods to support the 15 foot-high palm thatch roof. It is all held together by nothing but vines and palm fiber rope; no nails, just materials brought in from the forest. Inside, for the members of the family, there is absolutely no privacy. The only way to find privacy is to make off into the forest. In a space just twelve by twenty-four feet, families all sleep together on low platforms with their heads to the walls and their feet to the center, warmed by a smouldering fire. The older girls, unmarried women and widows of the family sleep on mats by the side of the house that opens out onto the plaza, from which they can receive nocturnal visits from the men in the village, without disturbing the others. Young boys sometimes sleep separately on their own mats, but the little girls generally sleep close to their parents or in a little group together on platform beds. Over the entire family the senior woman, probably a grandmother, rules.

Until they can walk Xikrin babies sit in a palm fiber sling under their mother's left arm. The other loop of the sling goes over the mother's right shoulder so it is easy to shift the baby from breast to breast at feeding times. From his earliest moments the young Xikrin warrior is brought up leniently, gently, gradually. He can call on the affectionate care of his mother's sisters, whom he also calls 'mother', and who help nurse him, even giving him a dry breast as a pacifier if ever he seems to need it. Every Xikrin baby gets plenty of attention. As husbands and wives are not allowed to resume sexual relations until their youngest offspring can walk, births are well-spaced. The baby of the family is not quickly supplanted. Older children have to wait for attention until the baby has been satisfied; however, even up to six years old a child can demand his mother's breast for comfort, even if a later child has been born. Along with the continued breast-feeding babies are gently weaned on roasted yam and banana, but do not get solid foods until they are two.

Mothers frequently paint their babies' faces and bodies, to give them sensual pleasure, and put the child to sleep. They shave their baby's heads just like adults, shaving the forehead to the crown while leaving the side and back hair long, and on the edge of the shaved area they paint geometrical patterns. Babies' earlobes are pierced a week after they are born; first, rods, then plugs and finally strings of beads with a mother-of-pearl pendant, are put in to expand the hole. At the same time the father pierces his tiny son's lower lip, and inserts a short string of beads and attaches it to a shell plug between the lip and gums. Mothers also weave their children cotton arm and leg bands impregnated with an oily red paint, a color believed to foster growth, strength, quickness, health and vitality. As the children grow, their outgrown plugs, cotton bands and dried umbilical cords are kept in individual pouches. Later they are stuffed into the hollow of a hardwood tree to give them, by magic, the great strength of the tree.

Young girls dance together in the afternoon, but never with men. They are thought ready for sexual intercourse between 8 and 10 years old.

A mother, with her head shaved on top with sharp bamboo slivers, delouses her child – a necessary daily task.

As a boy grows older he not only becomes more independent; he is encouraged to be fierce and brave. His uncle who, rather than his father, is the ultimate disciplinarian scarifies his lower legs with fish teeth until the blood flows freely. This is to let out the bad in him and make him fiercer. When his mother wants to scare him into obedience she says, 'I'll call your uncle'. Fathers like to see their small boys exert their temper to defy their mothers; a large toddler may hit his mother with a stick to the amusement and pride of his father.

Some time between the ages of seven and twelve, the boy's ties with his mother's household are almost completely cut. His parents sit wailing in their house as a substitute father enters, paints the boy black to indicate that his life is changing and then leads him out from his mother's house into the men's house. Here he is to eat, sleep, play, join in ceremonies and undergo ordeals to develop his bravery. His chest will be massaged with the poisonous down of a stinging caterpillar or with a heavy paint alive with ants or wasps. In this community he also learns the tribal sports of hunting and warfare.

At puberty, an elder leads the youths out of the village to a carefully selected hardwood tree, against which the boys are ceremoniously hurled one by one, again to give them the strength of the tree. Then each young man is given a penis sheath, the one item of clothing that men wear. Subsequently, he will feel great shame if he is ever seen publicly without his tiny folded palm leaf cover. With this sign of physical maturity and his clipped hair allowed to grow long as a sign that he is sexually active, he is finally permitted to have sexual relations. He is now also expected to be able to use adult weapons; a wooden club, lances, bone-tipped spears, and full-sized bow and arrows. He has become a warrior.

His initiation into social maturity is carried out in a long, three to four month ceremony. During this the initiates are given a more important adult place to sit, and after the ceremony youths are considered socially mature, and can marry any girl they choose, although their symbolic brides are usually too young for real marriage. The Xikrin feel that only married people are mature, and only mature people can marry. The young are free to marry as they choose, and often a youth slips silently into a girl's family hut every night. He does not eat while there and tactfully slips away before dawn.

However, when his first child is born, he moves in with his in-laws. He hunts food for them, cuts down a forest plot for his wife's gardens, and fully supports her and the children. Nevertheless he has little prestige among her relatives and almost no say in family matters. He is accepted into his wife's family slowly as his children grow older and as his children have children. A grandfather is highly respected.

It is a way of life in which divorce is simple whether before or after the arrival of children. If a husband deserts, a mother and children will always be taken care

27

Xikrin Brazil

In the dry season Xikrin are on the move, hunting game and gathering wild fruit. This monkey is being roasted for the evening meal.

(Center) A man and boy dismember a tapir to share among relatives. The freshly cut leaves are their disposable dishes.

of in her sisters' and mother's home. The husband just returns to the men's house to live there a full daily life, except for the odd times he goes visiting the house of his mother and sisters. A man's world, apart from hunting and farming, is principally politics, ceremonies, sports, oratory, and warfare and centers around the men's house.

For Xikrin women, changes are more gradual. From babyhood, through puberty, marriage, divorce or widowhood to a position of senior authority over her household a woman will live throughout in the same house, which is always the domain of the senior woman.

Although it is between the ages of eight and ten that a girl is considered ready for sexual intercourse, long before this she may marry a much older man, a widower or divorcee. The husband, who will keep a secondary wife for sexual purposes, comes and lives in her mother's house and helps bring her up.

From this early adulthood until she becomes a mother, the girl has her hair clipped short and wears a sling of red cotton cords to indicate that she is sexually available. She eventually becomes one of the wives of the men's house and whether married, betrothed or single, must receive any youths and men who have gained their penis sheaths. If she tries to keep herself for one man, the whole men's house will have her in the woods to teach her a lesson. A Cayapo must be generous with everything.

At puberty the girl undergoes a marriage ceremony. After her first menstruation her older husband, a suitor, or a young man selected for the occasion by her mother, sends a boy to tell her to be prepared to receive him in the afternoon. He comes to eat with her, possibly several days in succession, by a fire in the plaza in front of her house. When couples are seen eating together, a present or future sexual relationship is inferred. Then the suitor declares his intentions by sending a sleeping mat to her house. That night he goes there to sleep beside her, although several nights may pass before the marriage is consummated, an act which must be witnessed by a kinswoman of the bride, usually her mother. The bridegroom leaves in the morning and walks to the men's house to announce his marriage formally. He returns that night to lie by his bride. Her mother covers them with mats and they remain there very quiet, avoiding movements, speaking in low tones and eating only the blandest foods. During life's transitions the attachment of the soul to the body is so weak that it might be broken if the persons involved do not remain quiet. This ceremonial seclusion continues day and night for several days. On the final morning all the bride's uncles and aunts assemble around the couple and jokingly lie under their own mats in imitation of the bridal couple. A few minutes later the mother uncovers the couple who are then bathed with water brought by girls the same age as the bride to symbolically wash away any vestiges of her unmarried status. The rite, though very personal, is not very binding. Only the birth of a child cements a

28

Manioc flour — a staple food — is spread out on banana leaves to dry in the sun. Then women will make it into cakes.

When not occupied with
fighting or hunting, Xikrin
men spend pleasant
afternoons weaving
baskets or sleeping-mats.

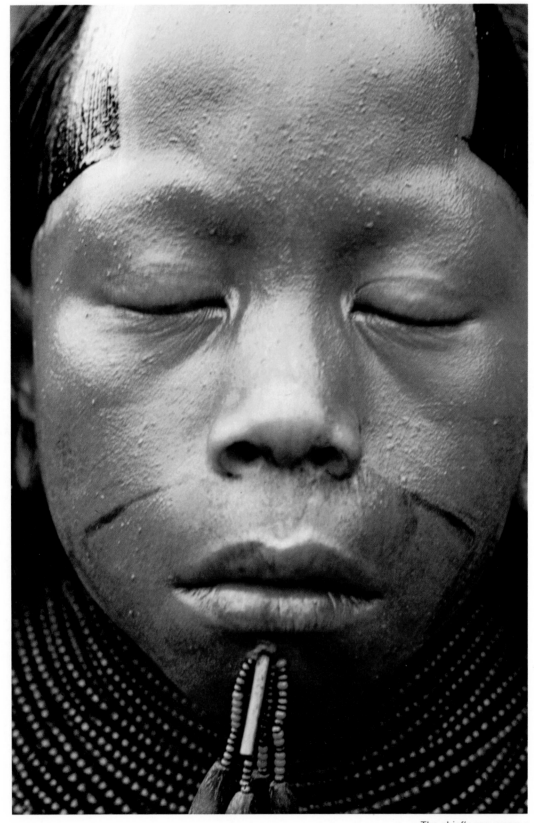

The chief's son wears a
lip plug and the Xikrin's
most precious ornament: a
necklace of black beads
and mother-of-pearl.

Father Caron — a Dominican missionary and the first non-Indian to have sustained contact with Xikrin — celebrates Sunday mass.

liaison into a real marriage.

For her initiation into full social maturity, a young woman is painted by a substitute mother to cut most of the ties with her real mother. She is now ready for child-bearing and is immediately admitted into one of the women's societies. As an adult there are certain ceremonies at which she must wail. Wailing is said to be touched off by the memory of deceased dear ones. A man who has reached this same stage of life is called upon to give extensive orations at the same rites.

There are some women who choose not to be formally married. They prefer to prolong their period of freedom and do so by a combination of contraception, infanticide and abortion and by maintaining their own farm plots. As their lovers will supply them with game, fish, and traded goods they are then economically independent of their mothers and sisters. Although some wives may view them with jealousy, they are not looked down upon by the community as a whole, and certainly not by men. A woman who has chosen to prolong her freedom can marry and become a housewife like the rest whenever she likes. But later she, like the other women and indeed the men, will gain prestige and respect as her children get married and have children of their own. Whereas the principal functions of the men's societies are political and social those of the women's societies are aesthetic and social: collective body painting. This painting is outstanding for the care with which various patterns, representing animals and natural objects, are applied to the body. For five or six hours at a stretch they paint on the designs, with fine palm leaf ribs or with their hands.

Death occurs, for the Xikrin, when the soul leaves the body permanently instead of temporarily, as it does during deep sleep, or when they are extremely frightened or in a coma. When a person appears to be dying, his spouse or kinsmen will try to revive him and prevent his soul from departing by beating the soles of his feet with switches, or by blowing smoke in his ears, or tickling the inside of his nostrils with feathers. If there is no response the person is clearly dead and must be treated as one treats the dead, wailing in the ritual manner and withholding food and water from the unfortunate patient who may still be quite conscious. As an officially dead person is already outside society and contact with him might cause further illnesses and more deaths, all relationships must be severed. Ghosts of the departed are known to be especially anxious for the ghostly company of their living relatives. Husbands and wives, especially, are the most likely to be haunted.

The corpse is laid on its back for up to twelve hours while mourning relatives sit around it and wail. Their singing-crying expresses and attenuates their feelings for the departed. They then place the corpse in a circular hole 3½ by 4½ feet deep with its knees flexed over its chest. The few possessions of the dead man are broken and deposited in the grave with him before it is covered up

with poles and mats with a mound of earth on top. The earth is left loose so the ghost can escape.

If a young child has died three months later the parents retrieve the child's bones and clean, wash, and paint them red. The red bones of the child are then hung from the roof inside the hut for three years or until an adult kinsman dies, when they are put with his corpse in his grave so that they can sleep together, and he can show the infant ghost the way to the villages of the dead.

The numerous Xikrin ghost villages are in caves under mountains. They can be detected by outcrops of the white rocks or white clay which ghosts are thought to eat. Ghostly life is very like the life of the living: ghosts hunt, fish, sing, dance, eat, grow up, marry and die just like living men. Their marriages produce no children and exist without tensions. Their village life is harmonious and free of conflicts: there is no warfare between ghost tribes. Eventually they pass peacefully away without trace. Still the Xikrin fear death and have a strong desire to live. The best thing about death is that it reunites kin and their loved ones.

31

Amahuaca
Peru, Brazil

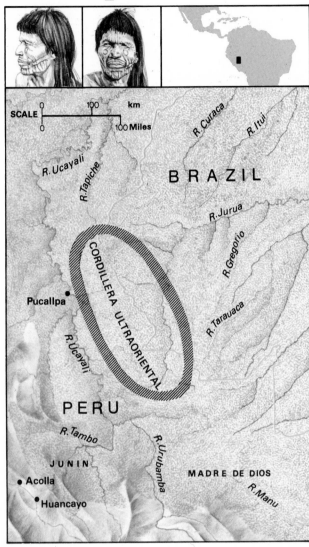

Human violence, more than any other single hazard, has reduced the Amahuaca tribe to a mere five hundred men, women and children. Today their survival is precarious. Their homeland, in the dense tropical forests of the Montana where the Amazonian jungle spreads over into Peru, abounds with danger from disease and animals. The pouncing 200-lb flesh-eating jaguar, the largest cat in the Americas, is but one of the Amahuaca's unfriendly neighbors. The venom of snakes like the fer-de-lance and bushmaster kills with notorious speed. Diseases, especially those brought by the white man, carry off many victims. But the greatest threat to the tribe's survival is the frequency of killings inflicted by the tribespeople on each other.

The Amahuaca woman goes off into the jungle, usually unassisted, to give birth. If she returns without a baby, no eyebrows are raised. Feeling that she cannot cope with the increase in her family she has strangled the

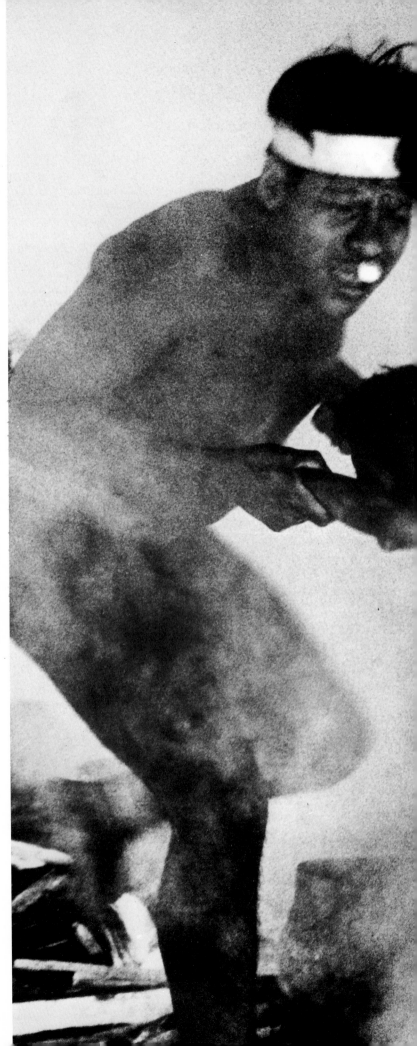

At an Amahuaca yearly festival, a young child is swung through the steam of boiling plantains — to make him big and strong.

34

Amahuaca harden their
sharply pointed arrows in
fire. They use them not only
to get food but as protection
against jaguars and snakes.

child within seconds of birth. The act is not considered murder, for a baby is not a social being till it has grown older. Girls are less useful than boys, and are therefore more frequently strangled.

Amahuaca usually have several wives. So the competition among men that polygamy always brings is sharpened by the scarcity of women. Jealousy arouses men to kill each other for women and worsens clan friction and fighting. And then there is the powerful hallucinogenic *ayahuasca* drink which sometimes inspires violent action.

A new-born child that is allowed to live is lavished with affection. It huddles in a sling on its mother's shoulders when she works in the clearings. It sleeps in her hammock for the first three years of life. Many children take milk from their mothers, or from other women in the extended family, right up till the age of eight. When the time comes to wean them, the mother resorts to rubbing the juice of fiery chili pepper onto her nipples.

Little boys are given small bows to play with and soon learn to kill with them. At first their prey is the lizard and tiny fish. Then they progress to squirrels and monkeys and fowl. When they can kill large fish, deer and tapir, they are considered fully-fledged hunters. They also learn to carve bows and arrows and the wooden clubs which they use to thrash their way through the jungle. They learn where to find honey, eggs and berries. And they pick up titbits of knowledge from the men's interminable hunting talk. They practise accurate stone-throwing, and mimicry to lure the animals and climb trees to track down game in the forest canopy.

But the Amahuaca also grow their food. They practise slash-and-burn agriculture. Every year they chop down some of the jungle and make a clearing (or *chacra*) where they can plant sugar cane, sweet-potatoes, squash, peanuts, maize, cotton, water-melon, tobacco, arrow-cane, plantains and their staple manioc. A *chacra* is productive for not more than three years. But there is no immediate problem – the Amahuaca occupy a vast area with an average of 20 square miles of land to every tribesman. Nevertheless white men who explored the Amahuaca jungle between 1890 and 1910 in search of valuable hardwoods posed a serious threat. However large its territory, no South American tribe today feels totally secure.

Although a tribesman's first allegiance is to his own family, the large tribal groups celebrate yearly plantain and maize festivals. A man who decides to hold a festival sings out his invitation to his friends and relations for several evenings before the event. When a prospective guest appears, an arrow headed with plantain leaves is thrown at him and he accepts by joining in the song.

When the plantains are ripe, the party begins. The men peel the plantains and begin to chew the soft flesh which they spit into containers. Meanwhile the women boil the hard cores and mash them together with the pulp masticated by the men. The singing together with the simple melodies of flute and bark trumpet never stops. The

children stand about watching. Then each child in turn is seized by two men and swung face down through the steam of the mixture. Next morning the men drink the concoction in great quantities and vomit it over the children. The yearly maize festival is like the plantain one – except that the maize soup is merely spat, rather than vomited, over the children. The process stimulates the development of the child into adult.

On such special occasions, people dress up. They sometimes wear high round hats and wide belts of seed. The hats have inner layers of bamboo wrapped in cloth soaked in the brilliant crimson *achiote* vegetable dye, which is primarily a cosmetic although it also wards off insects. Fashionable dressers sew black and brown seeds and monkey teeth onto their bark belts. A coarse red fringe of shredded fish – usually bass – masks their eyes like a veil. Round and round their waists they sometimes wind seed-strings which may be 40 yards long.

A premeditated killing is another occasion that calls for special dress. The man cuts off all his hair and covers himself from head to toe in *huito*, the rich purple-black juice of the genipap tree, before he marches off to encounter the foe. Usually Amahuaca clothing is extremely simple. The men, who are short and lithe, wear only a bark belt, and a ring in the nose. This was once made of a pearl shell, but now they use the aluminum of a crashed airplane. The women wear short cotton skirts and reed armbands. Men and women wear bark headbands which keep the hair out of their eyes.

The simplicity of their dress is balanced by the elaboration of their body painting. *Achiote* is daubed on as a base, while intricate patterns are sketched in *huito*. They often paint fearsome catfish and jaguar designs onto their faces and torsos, but most of the embellishment is for sheer beauty rather than symbolism.

While the men hunt, the women do the more humdrum chores. They collect water from the nearby Amazon tributaries. They collect firewood, they weave, grind the maize, plant and harvest the crops in the *chacras* once a year, and meticulously carve their weapons. But leisure is the norm, and it is a male privilege.

The prevailing langor of the men is punctuated by violent bouts of *ayahuasca* drinking. Women are very rarely allowed to join these sessions, which can last for four days and nights. Known to local whites as *soga de muerte* – the wine of death – *ayahuasca* has the effect of supercharged hashish. The drinker feels dizzy and numb, and starts chanting in an unintelligible falsetto. Blue flashes appear in the mind's eye, and experience and illusion take on a new dimension.

There is more than diversion to *ayahuasca*, for it is the gateway to the Amahuaca religious world. This is peopled by *yoshin*, spirits of the trees and of dead animals and people, who wander through the rainforest. They never rest. Usually they are hostile. They appear in dreams and impregnate women with malformed children 35

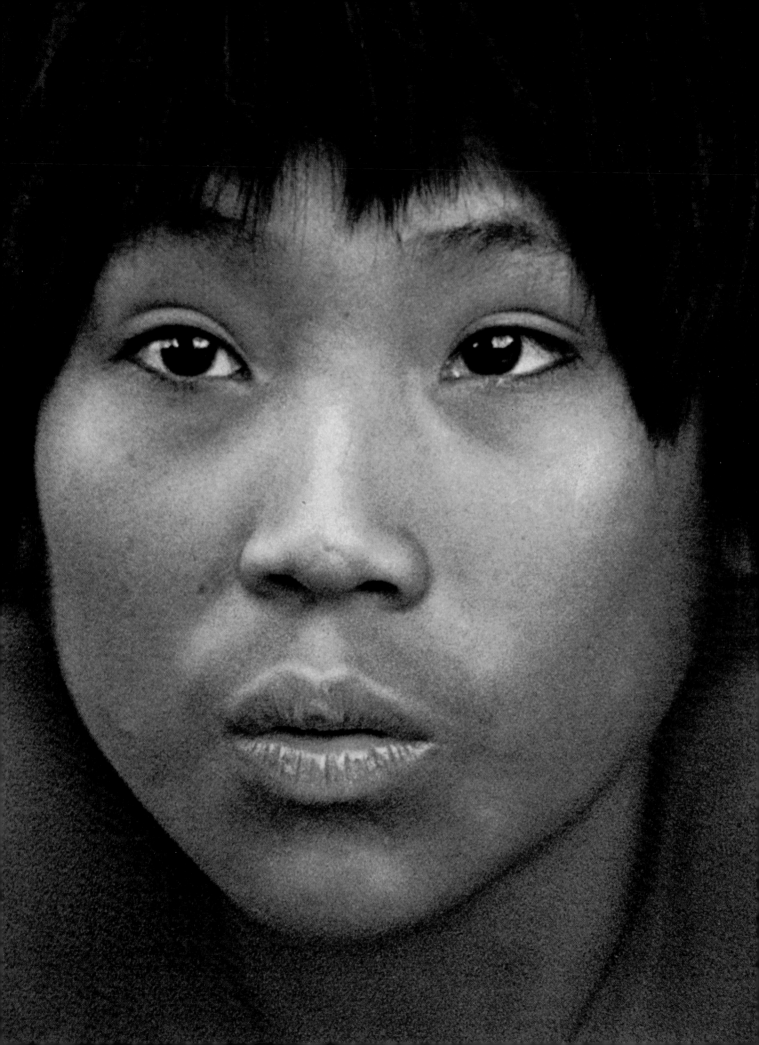

(Left) Twelve-year-old
Pansitimba carries the scars
of a vampire bat on his nose.
He already helps to support
his family by hunting.

who are called *yoshin vaca* (spirit-children) or afflict men
with nosebleeds or graver ailments.

But the *yoshin* can be friends. Their hostility melts
away if they are approached through *ayahuasca* and they
may tell men the secrets of the forest or give away the
adultery of unfaithful spouses. They warn of the prox-
imity of incorrigible wicked *yoshin* like those of the
anaconda, the electric eel or the carrion eagle, while the
king's vulture and the boa constrictor are potential
helpers. (Even in the world of reality, the boa constrictor
is a friend – a rub of its tail alleviates the sting of the large
black ant. But few obliging constrictors are ever found.)
Everything – animals, people, plants, minerals – has a
yoshin, but once a dead man has been buried his *yoshin*
ceases his restless wandering.

As well as the *yoshin*, there are various mythical figures
which children learn about from their parents. A hero
named Rantanga was supposed to have brought order
and prosperity to the Amahuaca tribe after a series of
disasters had almost wiped it out. Even today, Rantanga
makes his presence known when thunder rumbles: they
say Rantanga is clearing a new heavenly *chacra*.

In one respect the Amahuaca are unlike most other
tribes of South America. They regard the supernatural
and the mythical in a pragmatic – almost coldly objective
– way. While most tribes attribute accidents and misfortunes to witchcraft and malignant spirits, the Amahuaca regard them as coincidental. This facilitates the
fatalistic acceptance with which the Amahuaca face
shortening odds against their survival.

Nevertheless a man's death calls for elaborate guaran-
tees to ensure that the deceased progresses to a com-
fortable after-world. More important – in order to
preserve within the tribe the life-force of the dead man –
parts of his body are eaten by relations: the Amahuaca

are cannibals. If the deceased has died violently, his or
her body is cremated as soon as the next of kin arrives
on the scene. But usually the body is wrapped in the
clothing or hammock of the dead person. Then it is cremated after a week or more. The burnt body is taken out
of the clay pot in which it is cremated. The bones are
removed, washed in the river, ground into powder and
then drunk in a bowl of maize soup by the closest relation.
The cremation pot is finally buried with the ashes in a
grave dug in the floor of the relative's house.

Friends and relations wail and lament for the dead.
They sing long incantations about the life and goodness
of the deceased. Sometimes bereaved mothers keep up an
almost constant and voluble lamentation from the time
of the child's death until the drinking of the bone-powder
a week later. The drinking is considered a sorrowful and
rather unpleasant duty to be undertaken out of respect
for the dead and for the good of the tribe.

In 1947 the Peruvian government set up an outpost in
Amahuaca territory at Varadero. They were not there
to help the Amahuaca, but because they feared a
Brazilian invasion. In 1953, Robert Russell, linguist and
protestant missionary, settled near Varadero with the
aim of helping the tribespeople to survive. He has encouraged them to keep cows, but he has not brought
many material innovations into their life – their large
houses, big enough for a whole family, complete with
loom, hammocks and fire, are cosy enough. Nor has he
reacted with traditional Christian outrage at cannibalism. He does not order or preach, though he is convinced
that study of the Bible can benefit a people who are
culturally so different from his own. His main task has
been to persuade the scattered groups of Amahuaca not
to fight each other. Above all, he has tried to persuade
mothers not to strangle their new-born offspring.

Picking lice from a relative's
head is a daily task.
Except on special occasions,
men wear only a bark
belt around their loins.

An Amahuaca winds ropes of
clay into a pot for storing
ground maize. Corpses are
cremated in larger pots and
the ground bones are eaten.

Amahuaca clear the rain forest
by slash-and-burn, making
little clearings – *chacra* –
for sowing their manioc,
squash and other crops.

Jivaro
Peru and Ecuador

The practice of shrinking
enemies' heads grew up among
the Jivaro from their belief
that the spirits' power to
harm could be thus negated.

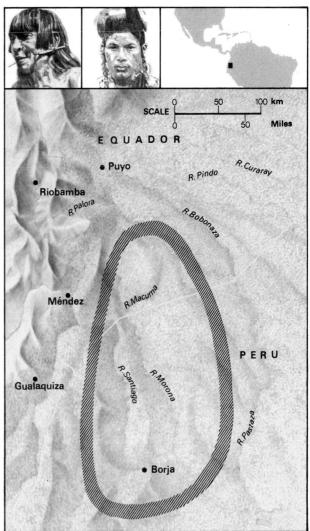

The Jivaro are at once among the most widely known and least understood of people. People have become aware of them because of their practice of shrinking the heads of victims taken in war. A complete explanation of the Jivaro's incessant warfare and its attendant head-hunting has yet to be given, but what is known about it is no less fascinating than the custom itself and can at least partly be understood through the Jivaro's own notions of their existence.

There are about 5,000 Jivaro, one of a number of Jivaroan-speaking peoples who live in a hilly terrain, covered with thick tropical rainforest, on the lower eastern slopes of the Peruvian and Ecuadorian Andes. Like most tropical forest peoples of the Amazonian forest, they farm by cultivating one patch of ground then moving on to another when it is exhausted. They also hunt, fish and gather forest produce. Although they can be divided into tribes and neighborhood groups, the

Jivaro normally live as a single family in an isolated and defensible house. Although one family may have close ties of kinship with neighboring families, their relationships are always tense and filled with suspicion. There is no formal political organization in Jivaro society, but during a period of hostilities a strong leader may temporarily weld together a number of families to fight. This ability to form temporary alliances appears to have been better developed in the past when the Jivaro were sufficiently united to ward off first the Incas and then the Spaniards. However today, years later, although deep inroads have been made into their territory, the Jivaro can still offer stern resistance to intruders. The famous case in point, during the last two decades, was their slaughter of a group of American missionaries.

However, even when the Jivaro are not menaced from outside, their lives are not peaceful. Their society suffers from endemic conflict, ranging from blood-feuds among local groups to wars of extermination between more distant tribes. It is not in the local blood-feuds but in the fighting between more distant tribes that the Jivaro take the heads of war victims to shrink.

When a successful raiding party has escaped with their trophy—the head of their victim—as soon as they feel safe from pursuit they stop and immediately begin the operation of shrinking the head, which takes about 20 hours. It is a technique about which the Jivaro are not at all secretive. They make a slit vertically down the back of the neck then pull the skin off over the skull. They scrape off flesh that is still sticking to it, sew the eyelids shut, and secure the mouth by three wooden pins held in place by string. They then immerse the head for two hours in a boiling herbal brew to reduce it by about one third, and to stop the hair falling out. Then they sew up the slit in the back of the neck. After the head has been filled with a succession of hot stones and finally hot sand, which helps to dry it out and further the shrinkage, the Indian molds and polishes its surface. When the head is fully shrunk he hangs it over a smoky fire for the night. In the morning he gives it a final polish, some decorations, and the *tsantsa* is finished. The raiding party continues its way home.

It is possible to gain an insight into the rationale of Jivaro raiding and head-hunting by examining their notion of what we can most adequately call 'soul' and they call *wakani*. The Jivaro believe that there are three kinds of *wakani*: an acquired soul (*arutam wakani*), an avenging soul (*muisak wakani*) and the true soul (*nekas wakani*). The true soul is, of the three, the one for which the Jivaro have the least concern although all possess one. It is the soul which departs at death, and, after a number of different existences, finally and forever becomes mist or cloud.

The *arutam* or acquired soul, however, never really disappears once it has come into existence. It may be roughly described as an ancestral ghost. The Jivaro

claim that the possessor of one *arutam* soul cannot die violently, while the fortunate possessor of two—the maximum possible—cannot die from any cause at all. An Indian is not born with an *arutam* soul: he has to acquire it before reaching puberty or he will not live for long. The acquisition of an *arutam* soul involves an ordeal for its seeker, who is sometimes little more than six years old. Accompanied most commonly by his father, the seeker makes a pilgrimage into the forest, to the nearest sacred waterfall which is believed to be the rendezvous of these souls. The souls wander about as breezes, scattering the spray of the long cascade. By day, the seeker bathes in the waterfall; by night, he sleeps in a simple lean-to. He fasts, drinks tobacco-water and awaits the appearance of the *arutam*. When the *arutam* appears, perhaps after five days have passed and the seeker has taken hallucinogenic *maikua* juice, the seeker, if he is brave, rushes forward and touches it with a small stick or with his hand. When touched the *arutam* explodes and disappears. This encounter gives the seeker the right and the ability to acquire the *arutam's* soul, which then passes into him. It is obvious to all when this has happened, as the young man's self-confidence and forcefulness increase greatly. A man who obtains an *arutam* soul is generally seized with a strong desire to

Other Indians have been quick
to exploit tourists, by
appropriating corpses and
copying the Jivaro method of
shrinking heads — for dollars.

kill, which he fulfils by joining a raiding party.

The evening before a raid, the members of the party are in a position to strike. They hold a ritual in which each warrior describes the *arutam* he has seen and which has possessed him. As each man does this, the soul departs his body forever to roam the forest—for *arutam* souls are satisfied with one killing. But in order to obtain another soul, the killing of the victim must very soon be successfully accomplished for the power of the departing *arutam* ebbs away gradually and in two weeks it is gone completely. If the raid on the intended victim fails, the party will seek out another victim to accomplish the necessary killing. When this is done the warriors return home and each immediately searches the forest for a new *arutam* with which he will regain immunity to violent death.

No Jivaro can possess more than two souls simultaneously, but possessing a second soul soon after the first has departed has the effect of locking in the residual power of the first. So a Jivaro who has made many killings can accumulate power. The *arutam* soul of a man who does not kill gets bored, however, and wanders off into the forest by itself where it may be captured by another Indian. A weak man who does not stand up for himself is seen as a man without an *arutam* and easy prey.

A man who dies violently must be without an *arutam* soul. On his death there come into existence his own *arutam* souls, equal in number to those he possessed during his lifetime, which go into the forest and in due course enter other Indians.

It is the same moment that the new *arutam* souls come into being that the third soul, the avenging soul *(muisak wakani)* is created. Only those who have acquired an *arutam* soul at some time during their life, and who die violently, give birth to an avenging soul. The function of the *muisak wakani* is to avenge the death of the person from whom it comes.

It is to imprison the avenging souls in the heads of their victims that the Jivaro shrink heads. The practice derives directly from the Jivaro belief in an avenging soul. This is why the heads must be shrunk as soon as possible after the raid. When the raiding party get back to their settlement they hold a series of rituals in which the *tsantsa,* the shrunken head, is the central focus. At the end of these rituals the avenging soul is expelled from the head and sent back to the region of its origin. Once the avenging soul is neutralized the *tsantsa* is no longer of any value or practical use to the Indians, and in the past it was buried or thrown out into the forest.

During this century, however, the Indians have discovered that there is a market for them and they are sold to local entrepreneurs and then shipped to the large cities for sale. And it is worth recording here that many of the shrunken heads for sale are merely the remains of hospital casualties that have fallen into the hands of professional if unethical taxidermists.

41

Flushed with triumph and
manioc beer, warriors return
with their shrunken head to
days on end of eating,
dancing and sexual license.

Xingu Brazil

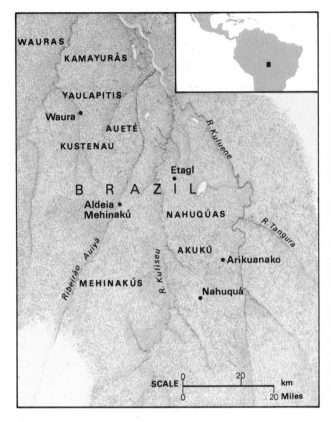

The seven tribes of the southern part of the Xingu National Park, which few explorers have ever reached, trace their origin from a pair of mythological twins—the sun and the moon. These two brothers were the children of the jaguar and his bride, a woman carved out of one of the towering jungle trees. The myth tells how the jaguar's mother, a giant moth, thought that she had been insulted by her new daughter-in-law and in a moment of anger when her daughter-in-law was pregnant, cut off her head. In his grief, the jaguar appealed to his grandfather, a leaf-cutting ant, to enter his dead wife's body and report on the sex of his unborn child. The grandfather ant returned with the news that in the womb were two male babies, both still alive. The twins were taken from their mother's body and recognized as the sun and moon.

Hundreds of myths are told and retold by Xingu tribesmen of the odyssey of these twins. They often tell of how the Xingu tribes were created: when each of the tribal chiefs sat before the sun and moon and was assigned an area of land for his village, and some specific knowledge and skill. To the Kamayura tribesmen, a 125 strong Tupi-speaking people, the sun and moon gave the knowledge of how to make the long, dark wood bow which they still use for hunting and fishing. To the Kuikuru, Kalapalo, Matipoo, and Nahukwa tribesmen, the sun and moon gave land-snails to be carved into belts

43

During the yearly flood, Wausha boys of the Xingu love bathing. They daub clay on their bodies to emulate their fathers' *urucu* body-paint.

Xingu tribesmen, like this Wausha, think ritual bleeding gives strength. Similar good comes from drinking tree poision, then vomiting it.

Bottom) Tribesmen use a dogfish's tooth as the razor with which they inflict ritual cuts on each other.

and necklaces that are today highly valued in Xingu trading ceremonies and often used in payment for wives. The myth goes on to explain how the chief of the Wausha (sometimes called Waura) was given clay and the secret of making the varied and imaginative pots in which all Xingu tribes prepare their manioc flour.

Today the Wausha tribesmen include the white man's tribe, the *Caraiba*, among those created by the sun and moon. All the Indian tribes were offered a rifle by the twins, but they did not realize its power and rejected it. When the white man was offered the gun he understood its meaning and took it for his tribe. The same mythical chief of the *Caraiba* watched the giant vulture circling in the sky with outspread wings and following the bird's example built the first airplane. From the movement of a duck's feet, the Indians say, the white man learned how to build an outboard motor and from the inner

A Wausha tribesman, covered in the paint of the *urucu* berry, clears the land. He paints a new pattern on his body every day.

After their first menstruation,
girls are secluded in a hut
for 3 to 6 years. Now they
emerge and offer the chief
nuts, symbol of fertility.

Xingu Brazil

Kamayura Xingu Indians approach the gods through sacred flutes, which a woman must never see — or she may be raped or even killed.

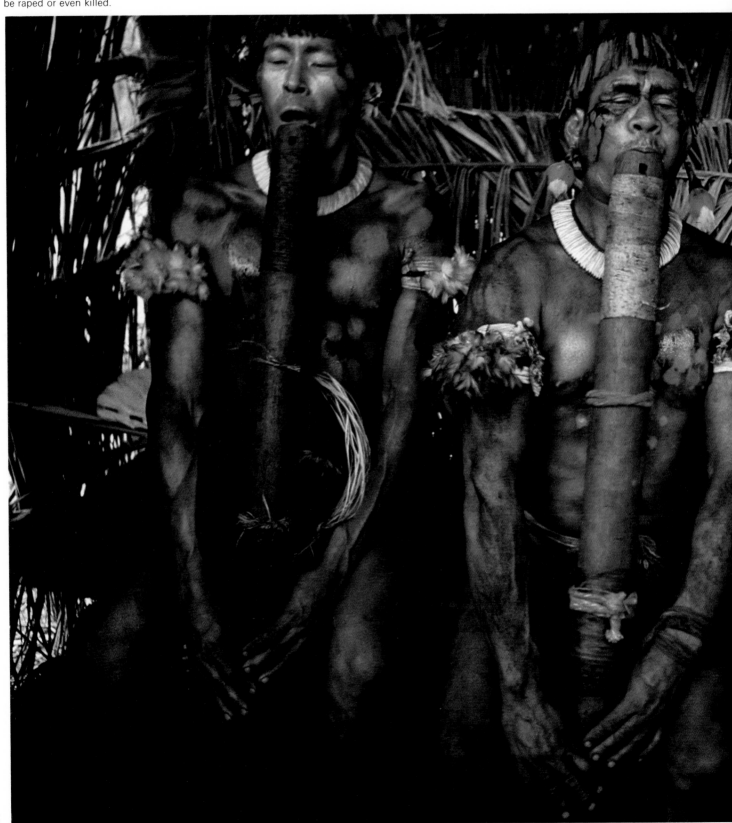

This chief of a recently contacted Xingu tribe wears a necklace of rodents' teeth and his face is caked with caterpillar cocoons.

47

The legendary brothers Orlando and Claudio Villas Boas have fought jungle and governments to create the Xingu National Park.

A Xingu boy archer holds
a silver otter. When
tribesmen shoot at fish and
water animals, they allow for
refraction of light in water.

made of wood, is also the symbol and voice of a spirit; men become spirits themselves when they play them. The flute spirit must be recognized, honored and fed if the Xingu tribesmen are to remain healthy and well-fed. They must be fed, above all, by the survivors of illnesses caused by the spirit attacks. When the flutes are not in use they are hung in a small, thatched house which women and girls are forbidden to enter, in the center of the circular village plaza. The woman are warned that they must never look upon the flutes themselves. When the flutes are about to be played the women shut themselves in their large, haystack-shaped family houses. If a woman should accidentally see them when they are played in the open, or is forced by the men to look at them, she may be raped and ostracized by the tribesmen.

Curing people is the responsibility of a specialist, or shaman, who is often a tribal chief and may also have been trained to use botanical medicines. A few greatly respected men attempt to convince the spirits to restore the health of the dying person by using tobacco-induced trances to enter the world of the spirits. They say a body's shadow has been stolen by the spirits; the shaman must return it to the body of the sick man if he is going to recover.

If someone of chiefly birth does die, his kinsmen may call for a funeral or *kuarupe*. Before the ceremony, several months after the death, they have to plant, harvest, prepare and store the masses of food which will feed the other Xingu tribes who will be invited to join the mourning ritual. Large silos are filled with manioc flour; jungle fruits are collected; salt is extracted from the ashes of water-hyacinth leaves and roots; and fish are trapped or shot.

In late August, after the first rains, a series of messengers, painted black and wearing bright yellow feathers in their ears, are sent to invite the neighboring tribes, who have barely 24 hours to reach the host tribe's village. Men, women and children travel quickly and silently down the rivers and through dense jungle, and arrive at dusk. They are directed to small clearings prepared for them in the jungle around the host village. The traditional Xingu hammocks are hung from the trees and both men and women paint themselves with red *urucu*, carbon, sweet smelling tree saps and pungent fruit oils. The men frequently bleed themselves with razor-sharp dog-fish teeth stuck with resin or wax to a wedge of dried gourd shell. The Xingu Indians feel that removing blood increases bodily strength and size. So does tightly binding the body, and drinking, and then regurgitating, very large amounts of poisons.

Just after dark each visiting tribe runs into the firelit village of the mourners and sees a line of tree trunks, painted and decorated with feathers, that represent both the chief who has died during the year and other non-chiefly tribesmen whom their relatives are commemorating. The mourners sit before the funeral tree-posts and

spiral of a snail's shell the white man learned how to build houses which soar into the air without falling over. All the Xingu tribes continue to specialize in those objects imparted to them by their mythical ancestors.

When a Xingu Indian is wearing his shell ornaments, a crown of eagle and macaw feathers on his head, and toucan feathers in his pierced ear lobes, and when his body is covered in red *urucu* seed paint, then he feels at ease with the world and walks and acts with assurance and dignity. But when he is without his shell belt and necklaces and his body is unpainted, he feels awkward, embarrassed, naked rather than nude.

A Xingu woman also paints her body with red *urucu*, but instead of a shell belt she wears several strands of palm fiber about her hips with a single strand which passes between the legs and holds a small triangle of white tree bark just above her labia. Around her neck she wears beads or sometimes a shell necklace that has been given to her either by her father, her husband or an admirer. There are female as well as male Xingu chiefs; the female chiefs are traditionally tattooed with small blue lines on their waists, shoulders and thighs.

The men of the Xingu are highly skilled musicians whose repertoire of flute music sometimes exceeds 100 different tunes. The flute, which is nearly 4 feet long and

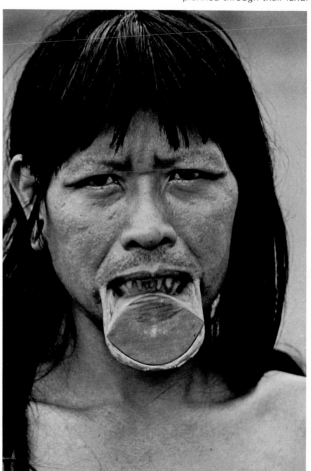

wait; the host and visiting tribes dance and chant around them. The dance ends as the visiting tribespeople dash up to the funeral posts and snatch a burning piece of wood from the mourners' fire.

At dawn next day, a wrestling tournament is held between the host and guest tribesmen. Then food is distributed to the guests, many of whom have not eaten for more than a day. Finally, long awaited, the secluded girls emerge.

When a girl in the Xingu menstruates for the first time she traditionally falls to the ground and is carried to her father's house. She lies perfectly still in her hammock, fasting and silent, until her menstrual period is over. She is then led into a dark corner of the house. She is surrounded by partitions of bamboo and woven mats and usually remains there until the next funeral *kuarupe*. Some girls, usually the daughters of chiefs or protective fathers, remain for two or three years in seclusion. Adolescent boys must also spend several years in seclusion. The southern Xingu tribes believe that the transition from adolescence to adulthood is a dangerous period, when you must be protected and cared for.

The entrance of the secluded girls into the village plaza is an exciting moment in the *kuarupe* ritual. Out they come, beautifully adorned with the family's shell belts and beads, from the windowless village houses. Their bodies are white and corpulent from months of seclusion and inactivity; cotton yarn has been tightly wound around their swollen legs. Precious yellow feathers have been woven into their long black hair which covers their eyes as it has not been cut since the first menstruation. They are now marriagable women, and they walk before the chiefs of the visiting tribes placing before each a handful of *pequi* fruit nuts that symbolize the fertility and sexuality of these girls now returning to tribal life as women.

In the northernmost section of the Xingu Park live the traditional enemies of the southerners. In past years *kuarupe* ceremonies were held to honor the dead killed in battle between them. The largest of the northern tribes whose cultures differ from those of the southerners, is the Txukahamai. Like the neighbouring Suya, the Txukahamai are a Ge-speaking people who wear lip disks and live more by hunting and gathering than by the fish and manioc diet of the southerners.

The Txikao, a semi-nomadic Carib-speaking tribe, long an enemy of the other Xingu tribes, have recently been peacefully contacted by the legendary brothers, Orlando and Claudio Villas Boas (the directors of the Xingu National Park), and encouraged to set up a village in the southern half of the reserve. Many nomadic and hostile tribes still roam the forests of the Upper Xingu river but, like the newly contacted Kreen-Akrore (see page 54), they must be befriended and given protection from the onslaught of road builders and settlers.

(K.S.B.)

The 15 tribes now in the Park are but a small portion of the tribes of Brazil, but they are unique in their variety and in their relationship with each other. There are seven distinct language groups. All the Indians would face extinction but for the Xingu National Park. Created and run by the Villas Boas brothers, it is a rare attempt to recognize and protect the dignity and rights of tribal people in Brazil.

What is remarkable about the Indians of the Xingu National Park is that here change is not forced upon them; they have been given time to come to terms with a materially superior society without being told at the same time that theirs is innately inferior. They are encouraged to work and live as they always have, but gradually to acquire whatever tools they find useful: they do not have to make a hurried choice between their culture and ours. Missionaries and tourists are excluded from the Park and only a few doctors and anthropologists are allowed to work and carry on research there. Groups of prospectors and trappers who enter have their guns confiscated and are made to leave, while the dangers of their presence, both to themselves and to the Indians, are pointed out. The Indians are free to leave if they wish and several have visited Brasilia and São Paulo for hospital treatment, to work for a time, or from pure curiosity. All, when they return say they cannot understand how anyone can find the western urban way of life superior to theirs.

One of the first things which strikes a visitor to one of the Upper Xingu tribes is the lack of a sense of nakedness. The Indians' bodies glow with vitality. Where the concept of shame has not been instilled it seems hard to believe that any mind, however puritan or salacious, could find the sight offensive.

In 1945, a government expedition led by the then three Villas Boas brothers traversed the region. They came to open up the area for development. But when they saw the beauty of the Indian way of life and the toll taken by disease they turned back to the Xingu and decided to build their first outpost. When their departmental chiefs allowed Indian land to be sold the brothers opposed them and fled to the jungle. They founded another post for the Indian Protection Service, but again had to flee from its corruption. Finally, Xingu was created a National Park and the Indians' right to their own land was officially recognized as theirs for ever.

A shaman leans over a sick man to dispel the disease by sucking the evil spirits out of his body.

Modern medicine in the
Park is slowly replacing the
shamans. A boy here
experiences the ordeal of
going to the dentist.

51

A Xingu tribesman
peacefully builds his house.
But for the Park, all
the tribes would soon
be extinct.

Tribesmen dam streams, put
poison in the drying lake
below the dam, then scoop
out the paralyzed fish.
Rewards are plentiful.

When the law to create the Park was eventually passed, only 22,000 square kilometers of land were included in it—less than a quarter of the area originally proposed. For ten years the brothers consolidated their work and, although funds were always desperately short and political pressures a constant threat, their medical campaign halted the epidemics and the population began a slow but steady increase.

In the spring of 1971, a road (the BR80) was driven through the center of the Park. It had originally been planned to go around the northern edge of the Park through largely open country. The Villas Boas were not consulted when it was suddenly diverted through the dense forests inhabited by the Txukahamai. Inevitably there were clashes between the Indians and roadworkers. Claudio Villas Boas had to try to explain to the shocked Indians that not all *Caraiba* (or white men) come with respect for the Indians' ways, that many are only interested in their women as prostitutes and do not believe that the Indians are really human. Ironically, the Txukahamai,

52

Equipped with *timbo* poison from the bark of a tree, Xingu tribesmen set off on a fishing expedition.

(Bottom) Just below the dam wall of bamboo and reeds, paddling tribesmen wait for poisoned fish to come to the surface, then scoop them up.

who would have attacked the roadworkers or fled from them a few years ago, now greet them as friends. They cannot understand why the newcomers abuse them and refuse them medicines they are accustomed to receive freely at the Post.

In 1971, a Presidential decree removed much land north of the BR80 from the Xingu National Park and put it on the market. In return, land to the south and west was added. It was claimed that the Indians were being given more land than they were being denied. But the land they had lost is dense, tall forest, the traditional homeland of the Txukahamai, while the new land is worthless open swamp on which no Indians could live. Around the edges of the Park live six or seven so far uncontacted tribes, with probably rather more Indians among them than those already living in the Park. The most urgent case is undoubtedly that of the Kreen-Akrore, whose territory is now surrounded.

The Brazilian government appears to ignore the lessons which developed nations have learnt too late: uncontrolled exploitation of natural resources can be fatal. The Indians—the supreme conservationists—hold many of the keys to how the jungle can best be utilized. Unless the Park survives, tragedy will befall not only the people but also a whole vast and rich region. (R.H-T.)

53

Kreen-Akrore
Brazil

There is an age-old myth in Amazonia that in the central Brazilian wilderness there is a tribe of timid giants. The first sign that these people actually existed came in the early 1960s when a young scientist attached to a small expedition in search of the headwaters of the Iriri river was attacked and killed by an unknown group of Indians in a region where no Indians were thought to live. It was an accident which was to lead to the discovery of the Kreen-Akrore people, and the realization of the myth.

At about the same time some hunters of the long-haired Txukahamai tribe who live near the region also had an encounter with the people they call Kreen-Akrore – 'people with the short hair': nobody knows what the Kreen-Akrore call themselves. In a skirmish with these people whom they regard as their enemies the Txukahamai captured a small Kreen-Akrore child. Here was living proof that in the vast jungle of Central Brazil there were entire tribes who lived and flourished in ignorance that they were not the only people in the world.

When the Brazilian government decided to build the Trans-Amazon highway it became important to tell the Kreen-Akrore about the outside world. They would have to be found and persuaded to move to the lands set apart for them by the Brazilian government. First to try to find and pacify the timid giants, the Kreen-Akrore, were the two Brazilian brothers, Orlando and Claudio Villas Boas, creators of the Xingu National Park.

The dense cover of jungle trees and vines makes the small Kreen-Akrore houses – rudely constructed huts with banana leaf roofs – almost impossible to detect from the air. From their small plane the Villas Boas brothers eventually sighted a single village with a garden that was so extraordinary and unexpected that it confirmed that the Kreen-Akrore, apart from rumors of their great height, were indeed quite different from the less isolated tribes of the same region. Most tribes of central Brazil practise slash-and-burn agriculture, planting crops at random in irregular plots claimed from the jungle by felling the larger trees in the rainy season and then burning the ground cover when it is dry. But the Kreen-Akrore had planted bananas and exceptionally tall corn in elegant geometric patterns that suggested the classical forms of French gardens. These strange impressive gardens showed that the Kreen-Akrore were clearly no long-lost off-shoot of their non-agricultural neighbors, the Txukahamai.

The Villas Boas brothers set out by boat for the newly discovered village in the early summer of 1968 to make contact with the Kreen-Akrore. After struggling up the river and through dense jungle for several months the expedition reached the heart of Kreen-Akrore country where they made a base camp on the banks of the Peixoto Azevedo river and a small landing strip for flying in food supplies. They built canoes, hollowed out of the massive trees that edge the river, to carry men and supplies to a point on the river nearest to the Kreen-Akrore village. In the event of attack the canoes would afford protection and escape, as it was thought that the Kreen-Akrore neither made canoes nor knew how to swim. The members of the expedition were given guns but carefully instructed never, even if they were attacked, to fire at a Kreen-Akrore, but to aim into the air. The brothers knew that just the sound of a gun was enough to frighten the unaccustomed into flight.

The guns were never needed, for at the beginning of the rainy season when the expedition finally reached the Kreen-Akrore village they found there no hostile enemy. The village was empty, desolate. For weeks the Indians had probably been watching the advancing expedition from their hiding places and had chosen to withdraw deep into the jungle.

The Villas Boas anticipated that the Kreen-Akrore would eventually return, and left signs in the village that they had come in peace. In the hastily deserted banana-leaf huts they left knives, machetes, steel axes, aluminium pots, matches, mirrors and, specially for the women and children, small dolls, combs and toy airplanes which they tied to the trees. Toy airplanes help to reassure Indians about those shiny steel birds they see crossing the skies and incite their curiosity about them. And ever since the brothers almost lost their lives when making friends with the Txukahamai, they have never neglected to provide special gifts for women and children. Their failure to do so not only upset the Txukahamai women and children; it infuriated their husbands and fathers.

Although the Kreen-Akrore did eventually return to their village nobody saw them. They took the gifts under cover of darkness exchanging them for offerings of monkey-meat, and arrows, clubs and stone axes. The clubs were beautifully carved and decorated, and so huge that only very big men could wield them. Whereas most central Brazilian Indians average a mere five feet, the Kreen-Akrore are certainly over six feet tall and not much below seven. The expedition left more presents, waited for the Kreen-Akrore to come back, but had to return as its supplies dwindled and the Amazon tributaries flooded as the rainy season reached its peak.

Three years later the Villas Boas brothers, now nearly 60 years old, set out once more to meet the Kreen-Akrore. This time they spotted two villages from the air. The larger one had 14 houses and 56 gardens. They observed that the Kreen-Akrore sleep close together inside their wall-less houses, and they calculated the population of the two villages in hundreds. Their planes flew low and they dropped more presents. The Indians shot arrows at the planes, but seemed pleased with the presents. From these planes were taken the very first photographs of the Kreen-Akrore.

Once again the Villas Boas brothers cut their way through the jungle and camped outside the smaller village. Presents were exchanged. The Indians never once

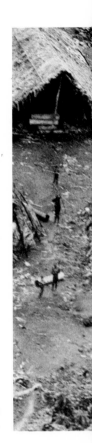

No outsider has ever met the Kreen-Akrore tribe. It has managed to evade the white man, but unless contacted it will probably die out.

(Top) Strange logs—apparently not for burning—lie around the houses. The size of clubs and hatchets suggest that they are very big men indeed.

(Bottom) Wigwam-shaped graves and elaborate geometric designs for the gardens indicate that the tribe is quite unlike its neighbors.

The only living proof of the Kreen-Akrore's existence: a small boy, with one of his Txukahamai captors.

allowed themselves to be seen. But they certainly watched every move in the expedition camp. The brothers would probably soon have been invited into the village, had not a member of the highway survey team been so surprised in a sudden encounter with some Kreen-Akrore in the jungle that he fired on them, shooting, possibly killing, one of them. Within a few hours the entire tribe had deserted their village and disappeared once more into the jungle. The disappointed brothers had no choice but to reach the larger village. By the time they got there it was burned and deserted. The Kreen-Akrore had retreated into the jungle.

At the time of writing, the Kreen-Akrore are homeless and surrounded: in one direction lies the Villas Boas camp; in another the broad Teles Pires river which is impossible to cross without canoes or swimming ability. From yet another direction comes the new road and the new settlers, accompanied by Brazilian soldiers. Even if the Kreen-Akrore cross the river, they will enter a region of hostile tribes, settlers and prospectors. The Kreen-Akrore, like dozens of other isolated Amazonian tribes, have a bleak future.

55

The exploitation of Amazonia

The cold-blooded killing of defenseless Indians by gangs of white men has long accompanied the exploitation of the jungle. During the 1960s there certainly were widespread killings in the Brazilian states of Amazonas, Rondonia and Mato Grosso. There is little to suggest that the killings have entirely stopped.

'Civilized' men, lonely, frightened, frustrated, under the strain of the pioneer's life in the jungle, can easily turn into savages. Once Indians were only occasionally killed – in self-defence. Soon killing was not always a necessity; it was almost a sport.

Lucien Bodard, for example, in his *Le Massacre des Indiens,* describes a scene of slaughter that was common in Amazonia – and can still occur. In the 1960s a professional gang led by Chico Luis exterminated with machine guns the Cintas Largas tribe of the Rio Aripuana in the Brazilian state of Amazonas. The pleadings of old women, the sobs of children, fell on deaf ears. Girls were raped. The killers laughed. Before the first European explorers arrived in 1500, the enormous country of Brazil – larger than the United States without Alaska – was thinly populated by indigenous peoples of uncertain origin. Disease, warfare and starvation drastically reduced the numbers of those Amerindians of the coastal region who took the full impact of the colonizer. But in the least accessible parts of the country, those tribes which specialized in jungle-dwelling were to survive for centuries largely undisturbed. Today, as the jungles of Amazonia and Rondonia and the Mato Grosso are more intruded upon, their survival is gravely challenged.

Their origin has been explained by various theories of a semi-mythological kind and, more seriously, by suggestions that they are of relatively-recent Asian or Polynesian origin. They certainly look somewhat Asiatic, with their straight, black hair, relative lack of facial and body hair, stocky physique and the epicanthic fold above the eye. Nevertheless, affinities with Chinese and other eastern languages should not be taken too seriously.

Whatever their origin, the Indians are declining rapidly and the white man is clearly to blame. When he first came to the territory which is now Brazil there were some three million Indians living there: by 1964 there were about 200,000; there are only half as many today.

The most innocent but most important reason for their decline is disease. Tough, hardy and able to thrive in an environment which by European standards is nightmarishly hostile, the Indians are nevertheless highly susceptible to white men's illnesses, even to those which are relatively mild elsewhere, such as measles and influenza. Even today, isolated groups can be decimated following the friendly visit of some European who happened to have a feverish cold.

Their numbers have been reduced by the mere impact of civilization. Many tribes have been uprooted from

Prospectors, miners, timber
men and land buyers spearhead
the invasion of Amazonia. The
result — like the diamond
digger's shack — is ugly.

The exploitation of Amazonia

This diamond-digger spends the day down a waterlogged hole near a post in a part of the forest from which the Indians have been driven out.

It is in Indians' territory that *diamanteros* like these search for gems. Frequently the shy Indians are killed, evicted or otherwise broken.

A diamond-diver stands ready for exploration along the bed of a little-known Amazon tributary deep inside Indian territory.

their home regions, and, with their traditional way of life made impossible, forced into starvation. Extreme malnutrition, coupled with defeatism and psychological disorientation, are now widespread. Many groups of Indians seem to have been deprived of the will to live.

The third reason for this decline is simple genocide. The Indians are dying out because they are being killed off.

There is nothing new about this; nor is it without parallel in the western hemisphere. The activity of the professional 'Indian hunters' can be seen in perspective, though no more favorably, as the last phase of a widely-accepted colonialist tradition in the Americas.

In the early part of this century, the enormous demand for rubber brought great prosperity to Brazil, and the town of Manaus – as the center of the trade – became a wildly picturesque boom-town after the style of North American gold-rush settlements. Very little of this prosperity reached the seringueros, the wretched near-slaves who actually gathered the rubber, living and working alone in the deep jungle.

The Indians were understandably hostile to the white strangers who invaded their territory, driving them ever deeper into the forest in their rapacious search for wild rubber, diamonds and gold. The prospectors tended to work singly or in small groups; they were vulnerable to ambush and stealthy attack from the forest gloom. Many of them fell to Indian arrows. The prospectors and the trade itself had to be protected from the arrows and clubs of the Indians, and the obvious steps were taken.

Later, when Malayan competition had almost ruined the Brazilian rubber trade, the hostility of the seringueros towards the Indians was continued by the garimpeiros, the countless prospectors for diamonds and gold. Poor and often hopeless men of mixed origin and often with some Indian blood themselves, true garimpeiros have seldom struck significant success in their hunt for metal and stones. Like all other European and semi-European developers of Brazil's jungle resources they have always seen it as their first and necessary task to get rid of the

local Indians. And so began the continuing process in which vigorous European self-defense developed into a policy of exterminating the local Indian population as a necessary preliminary to the occupation or development of an area. With certain local eruptions this process continues.

At the simplest level it has involved mounting Indian-hunting expeditions, well armed with rifles and machine-guns. More subtly, infected garments and poisoned food-stuffs have been distributed in simulated friendship. Indian villages have been bombed with light aircraft and attempts have been made to foster inter-tribal wars. Wholesale death has been inflicted upon these indigenous people in one way or another complete with wholesale torture, rape and every kind of atrocity. 'Genocide' is not too strong a word. The white man's manifest destiny has been regarded as fully justifying the principle that in this situation, 'might is right', although it has some-times been rationalized on the pretext that the Indians are in fact sub-human, or alternatively that their alleged cruelty, cannibalism and vice put them beyond the pale.

In Brazilian government circles and elsewhere mis-givings have been felt about it. But in so vast a country, where government has often been corrupt and where communications have until recently been bad, it was never easy for central authority to control distant events, nor to act against the powerful commercial interests developing the country regardless of cost in Indian lives.

The Indians have had their defenders. The most famous of these was Candido Rondon, himself partly Indian, who died in 1956 aged 91, after receiving the Nobel Peace Prize for his attempts to establish peaceful relations with the Indians. He was instrumental in founding a governmental agency, the Service for the Protection of the Indians (SPI), to look after their interests. This was a substantial step in the right direction.

Rondon died – perhaps fortunately – before it became clear how completely the SPI failed to live up to his ideals. It was inadequately financed, staffed by the wrong type of people, and in 1968 the Brazilian government had to admit that it had become a sinkhole of corruption and indiscriminate killing, and had connived – to put it mildly – at wholesale theft and massacre. Dismissals followed and later the SPI itself was dissolved to be replaced by the National Indian Foundation (FUNAI).

The declared objectives of the foundation included respecting Indian people and institutions and guarantee-ing them permanent possession and use of land and natural resources. They turned out in the end to be empty promises. In 1972 Antonio Cotrim, a leading defender of the Indians, resigned from FUNAI, condemn-ing it as an instrument of government hypocrisy and the grave-digger of the Indians. At about the same time, General Bandeira de Mellor, the President of FUNAI, while proposing various measures for the Indians' **59**

The result of perhaps two long months under the severe hardship of life in the jungle: a handful of rough diamonds.

The exploitation of Amazonia

Latex — from which rubber can be made — is smoked till it coagulates into balls, which tappers and collectors here weigh.

Relentlessly dividing virgin forest, the Trans-Amazon Highway is the pride of 'progressive' Brazil — to the Indians a desperate challenge.

This man's garb protects him from mosquitoes. The malaria they carry is the chief enemy. White intruders must also beware hostile Indians.

At the outpost of Capori, pioneers have hacked an airstrip out of the forest. Its impact will be felt for 50 miles around.

Countless adventurers have
been drawn to the Orinoco
and Amazon in search of
gold. Almost all have ended
up surviving by panning.

welfare, insisted that economic considerations came first: 'we must not let an isolated minority impede Brazil's progress'.

At the time of writing, the Trans-Amazon Highway, Brazil's great symbol of progress, destined to extend for 3,350 miles from the Atlantic coast to the Peruvian border, is under construction. Running through some of the world's most dense and inhospitable jungle country, this highway will certainly open up the central regions of Brazil and encourage the exploitation of immense mineral resources. Even so, weighty economic and environmental arguments have been brought against the project. It seems likely to put many of the remaining Indians in a finally impossible position, destroying their isolation and their way of life, forcing upon them a white civilization to which they have never been able to adapt, leaving them with the prospect of illness, alcoholism, despair and death.

Meanwhile, a valiant effort still continues to maintain them and their traditional style of living. Since the early 1940s, the two brothers Orlando and Claudio Villas Boas have lived among the Indians, studying their languages and customs, helping them medically and economically, and defending them where possible from white hostility. In 1961 these efforts were officially recognized when an

area as large as Ireland in the state of Mato Grosso was designated as the Xingu National Park, a reserve within which the Indians could live undisturbed. Orlando Villas Boas was appointed as its director. But even his spectacular energies could not prevent the driving of a highway right through the park, and the consequent death of many of his Indian people.

As he describes them (and he probably knows the Indians as closely and sympathetically as any other man alive) they are an essentially *good* people, psychologically adapted to themselves and to the frightening world around them, who need no total gods nor equivalent patterns of worship, and are therefore unrewarding material for the Christian missionary. They do have myths and fantasies of evil. They believe in spirits which can perhaps be equated with their own fears, and they resolve the consequent tensions by songs and dances and rituals presided over by witch-doctors.

They live from day to day, taking a short-term view of their situation, and thus gaining in peace of mind what they lose in security. In large huts, thirty or forty couples, and all their children and animals, live together with little or nothing in the way of government, taking personal freedom for granted, and without chaos. Their hereditary chiefs or *caciques* are chairmen and masters of ceremony, 61

The exploitation of Amazonia

rather than rulers. They are fond of practical jokes and horse-play, but tradition and custom impose a high degree of reticence, restraint and self-control. Genuine quarrels and conflicts of interest are rare and soon resolved – by reconciliation or by a parting of the ways.

It is their instinct to do as little work as possible. The work they do is divided between the sexes. Anything connected with water – collecting it from the river, boiling the fish in it – is women's work. But smoking fish, and collecting wood for this purpose, is men's work, as is everything connected with the jungle, with animals, with hunting and fishing and the building of huts.

Except where European influence has begun to prevail (not very far, since the Indians find it easier to die than to adapt) their technology is limited to the stone axe and the bow, and their clothing to an unconcealing belt, which varies from one tribe to another in width and design. The effect of nudity is heightened in both sexes by the fact that they have no body-hair at all, but is mitigated by

The skeletons of slaughtered Indians are laid out for sale to timber-workers and tappers looking for souvenirs to take home.

At remote Santarem, on the 2,000 mile Amazon, whites buy rifles, for 'defense' against Indians, from a priest known as 'Bishop of the Amazon'.

In an upriver market a professional teller of tales reads a story of love and danger to illiterates who pay him for his pains.

At lonely, pestilential jungle posts there are few solaces: the bottle, a whore, and the luxury of a scratchy record-player.

widely practised tatooing and body-painting, especially in connection with certain ceremonies. For personal adornment, in some tribes the lower lip is enormously distended by the insertion of a large wooden disc.

The Indians live mainly on manioc, fish and the meat of wild animals, including alligators. They preserve the roots of manioc (cassava) by forming them into large balls, smoking these and then boiling them non-stop for several days. The finished product looks like a black cheese, and it keeps indefinitely. The Indians take a supply of these on their travels, softening them in water into a soft sticky paste and then cooking it into a kind of pancake. From manioc – once the poison has been removed – they also make alcoholic drink, which they leave in the open to ferment in big earthenware pots. Any passer-by is expected to help the process of fermentation along by taking a mouthful, mixing it with his own saliva, and returning it to the pot.

The Indians take marriage with a qualified seriousness. It is usually arranged by the parents, but with a boy often indicating his own preference: if he returns to the hut and finds that a girl's hammock has been slung beneath his own, he knows that he is married as from that moment.

An expectant mother is allowed to abort herself with herbs and drugs if she chooses. Among some of the tribes of the Xingu region, there is a traditional practice of limiting families to three children – the fourth and later children being killed at birth. With these qualifications, the Indians are extremely fond of children and cherish them with little regard for their often uncertain paternity, asking and expecting them to behave well, and usually with good results. To punish a child is rare and it is rumored that Colonel Fawcett, who mysteriously disappeared in the Xingu jungle in 1925, was killed by an angry father for slapping a child who had interfered with his belongings.

One should not idealize the Indians, or take a too idyllic view of their way of life: it is possible that the Villas Boas brothers, who have done so much for them, are excessively influenced by the 18th century myth of the 'noble savage'. Today at least, the behavior of the Indians often displays a kind of ambiguity between innocence and savagery. There is, for example, a tradition that when a young mother dies, the small children who depended upon her must be killed. Cruelty or compassion? Their claim is that since every young creature needs to have a mother, it is kindest to spare these children the burden of motherless existence.

But it goes further than this: in some tribes newborn twins are strangled, in others the old are buried alive, and in yet others carefully-chosen parts of a dead enemy are smoked and preserved so that they can be eaten later, at some tactically important moment.

By European standards, this is indeed 'savage' behavior. But within the tribe there is little cruelty; even the inter-tribal wars are modest affairs, soon settled without too much bloodshed. Only where the tribal territory is seriously threatened do they feel so strongly that warfare becomes more bitter and prolonged.

Their chief crime, it seems, has been their 'savage' defense of their homeland and culture from foreign invasion and exploitation. They had little chance. The Indian cannot adapt to white civilization: the most that he can hope for is to keep away from it, and this is becoming progressively more difficult. Now that his jungle-refuge homeland is being opened up by roads and airlines and developed by big business, his survival in isolation is even less likely.

Perhaps this opening-up will give the government in Brasilia a better chance to control what happens in those distant parts of the country: perhaps it will be realized that there is a moral case against genocide, and that economic development can be purchased at too high a price. But unless there is a radical change of heart and policy on the white man's side, the Indians of the Brazilian jungle are doomed.

63

Cities of lowland America

In the doorway of a massive, modern building in São Paulo, sleeps a negro, with his wife and child. It is their first night in town. They have trekked down from a village in the provinces. Next day they may make their way to the favelas, the towns of cardboard and tin on the hills outside the city. He may, if he is lucky, get a job in São Paulo, perhaps in a factory owned by someone of German or Italian Swiss descent. His wife too may, if she is lucky, become a domestic. She will buy her mistress' fruit and vegetables, and collect her mistress' laundry from a shop owned by someone of Japanese descent.

In the great cities of Brazil – São Paulo, Rio de Janeiro and Brasilia – most people are of immigrant stock. If they are not from the provinces, they have come from abroad: from Germany, Italy, Portugal, Spain; or perhaps they are Jewish. And there are 600,000 Japanese. São Paulo, a city of 6 million inhabitants, is the sixth largest in the world and is still growing. Brazil has one of the world's highest birthrates. For immigrants, it is the most magnetic of all Brazilian cities. The Portuguese and the Spanish came first to swell the middle-class, followed by Italians. If its present rate of growth continues, it will be the world's biggest city by 1984.

In the great Argentine city of Buenos Aires, where people tend to remark 'We are Italians, speaking Spanish, dressing like Englishmen', the influences are just as cosmopolitan, although the result is an essentially middle class city compared with the sharp contrasts between rich and poor in the cities of Brazil. Buenos Aires can rival New York as a home for the wanderers of the world. In the 19th century came the Italians and the Spaniards; early in the 20th century, three quarters of the population were immigrants, mainly from Europe. The British beef trade helped the town to grow and in 1972 it had a population of almost nine million people.

Argentina is a European country and feels it – almost excessively at times. Before the war it was booming and equal in prosperity to Canada. Then its Spanish-style *caudillo* cult, its desire for a strong personal leader, landed it with the dictator Juan Perón; its sense of woman's mystery with his wife Evita. The result was economic stagnation, a brain drain of some of its most promising young men including scientists, doctors and managers, and an envious, anxious awareness of its racially mixed neighbor Brazil – a country as vast as a continent without, as yet, a population to match. Gloomy Argentines now speculate on the impact of three hundred million Brazilians by the year 2,000.

The Brazilians sense their anxiety: 'They call us black monkeys' they say. The eye can be truthful up to a point. Sit at an outdoor cafe in São Paulo or Rio de Janeiro and watch the multi-colored crowds pass by: white, brown, black, quadroon, octoroon, and finer combinations still. They have the good humor for which Brazil rightly congratulates itself, and are visible evidence of inter-marriage of which it also boasts.

Mar del Plata, Argentina, the
largest seaside resort in
South America, draws thousands
of visitors from Buenos Aires,
200 miles to the north.

In Salvador, an elegant house
in the Portuguese style,
occupied by several families,
crumbles with neglect. Brazil's
poor have worse homes.

Oscar Niemeyer designed
Brasilia as a dream capital,
in concrete moulded like clay,
recalling Brazil's interior.
Residents find it unhomely.

Cities of lowland South America

The gambling instinct runs strong in South America. The world's largest casino, in Argentina's Mar del Plata, has 90 roulette tables.

To be buried in La Recoleta cemetery — a tiny city for the dead of Buenos Aires élite, with paved streets and street lamps — may cost $100,000.

In Brazil the 'bleaching' process, as it is called, began in the days of slavery. There were white masters and black slaves – many of them women – but practically no white women. And so there was every inducement for white men to have offspring by women slaves, and nothing to stop them. 'As a result of these factors' writes T Lynn Smith 'the genes of the upper-class white men have not only passed on to legitimate offspring who have remained at the top of the social pyramid, but they have contributed greatly to the "bleaching" of the darker population of the social strata.'

Brazil is some steps short of being a homogeneous, multi-racial paradise. In the great Brazilian corporations the management are more likely to be pale than dark. The whiter you are the higher your class. When, in an experiment, negro researchers went to register their children at expensive private schools, they were generally unsuccessful; white researchers, however, had no difficulty. And in another recent experiment, passers-by rushed to the aid of a white researcher who lay on a crowded pavement pretending to be ill. When a negro researcher did the same the crowds just walked round him. They said they thought he must be drunk.

Buenos Aires is the southern hemisphere's largest city — 'the Paris of South America'. It has been largely rebuilt during the 20th century.

Brazil is nevertheless basically liberal in its attitudes to race and color. The omens for racial ease are good. Politically it has tended to seek less extreme solutions than its neighbor Argentina. Although there is some resentment in the provinces of the power and bureaucracy invested in the big towns, Brazil has an adaptability and social cohesion that portend great possibilities of development. It also has odd affinities with two other great fast-developing nations, the United States and the USSR.

There are in Brazil, as in the United States (particularly in the west), flexible, immigrant entrepreneurs impelled by a sense of a pioneering tradition. In São Paulo there is a great monument to the Bandeirantes, the hard men who thrust into the interior of Brazil, capturing and killing as they went, who developed São Paulo from its beginnings in 1554 as a Jesuit mission station.

In Brazil great cities of stone have risen at the behest of immigrants and their sons and grandsons. Some sprang up, unfolding and growing of their own accord. In São Paulo today a new building is completed every hour. Others, like Brasilia and Belo Horizonte, were planned on the drawing board. Men and women, for whom the planners did not account, have trekked across hard, hostile country to become their citizens, often settling in favelas that straggle the edge of their furthest suburbs.

In these cities there is too a restless, shifting interest in the 'modern', not only in the fashions for architecture, but also in the sudden fickle passions for new develop-ments. A sudden craze for concrete poetry, for instance, will quickly die with the equally sudden shift to the next novelty. In industry, new United States or European management techniques are seized on, and not always adequately developed, by the time they are abandoned for the next, more novel, fad. But there is great thrust and great courage which is followed through often enough: Rio de Janeiro, São Paulo, Brasilia and Belo Horizonte have vital architectural achievements, as well as great buildings that seem inadequately finished.

It is the solid, bureaucratic weight of Brazilian government that overwhelmingly reminds one of Russia. The 19th century Brazilian novelist Machado de Assis, while nicely reflecting the entrepreneuring spirit in his *Epitaph of a Small Winner*, also conveys the country's bureau-cratic spirit in a way that recalls Gogol's *The Overcoat* and some of Dostoevsky's civil servants. Today the bur-eaucratic presence sometimes makes itself felt by the oddest rulings. A certain deputy for example, brought in a bill to prevent children being called God, Jesus or Jehovah. There is possibly no other country that has such a tension between the drive for innovation and the tradition of bureaucracy.

The need for play, for pleasure, and for sexual involvement, are also strong in the Brazilian psyche. Carnivals, television, films, newspapers, magazines, music and, above all, sport provide the semblances of arenas, of spectacles, of tragedy, musical emotion, death,

69

For Argentines, horse-riding is a national sport. In the members' enclosure at Palermo race-course, fortunes may be wagered on a race.

At Manaus, 500 miles up the
Amazon, the night is lit by
a thousand candles for the
Finados, the Catholic feast
of the Day of the Dead.

and aesthetic violence. The carnival spirit has a strong libertarian and democratic impulse, so that people may regard social and moral barriers as temporary and flexible. On the spirit of carnival, Almor de Andrade writes: 'it is a protest – a gigantic protest of delirious, mad multitudes against the formulas which separate them from each other, against all the artifices which the social order requires for the preservation of itself.' The great football arenas in Brazil create heroes unmatched by any pop singer, politician or artist. And Brazilian football, though hard, has not the fierce, masculine bitterness, the *machismo* element, of Argentina. It has grace, intense subtlety, and a histrionic appeal. To the Marxist it may be 'the opium of the people', temporarily deluding a mass of poor Brazilians into a feeling that they are millionaires. But it has provided millions with the most comforting of entertainments.

Fernando de Azevedo writes: 'The Brazilian is altruistic, sentimental, generous, capable of impulsive passions, violent but only slightly tenacious, loving life more than order, pacific, hospitable, suspicious, tolerant by temperament and by lack of concern. A hard worker endowed with vigorous individualism . . . of an imagination rich in fictions . . . irreverent, enamored of events and sensations . . . tolerance . . . the sentiment of patriotism is one of the living forces of the Brazilian.'

The Brazilian attitude to religion is rather like that of the ancient Romans: all kinds flourish, and the predominantly Roman Catholic population is tolerant to both Protestants and Jews. Negroes in Salvation Army uniforms go from café to café with the text for the day; there are spiritualist meetings to go to; walk on the early morning beach at Santos and you may glimpse chicken claws and entrails – relics of macumba rites. Paulo Prado, in his book *Retrato do Brasil*, says sensuality and envy are the two strongest characteristics. They are traits, he believes, which go back to the sexual passion which wore out the Portuguese and the Indians, and to the hunger for gold and the sadness of the African slave. Gilberto Freyre however, argues that the negro 'gave us a revelation of a kindness greater than that of the whites, of a tenderness such as Christians do not know, of a warm, voluptuous mysticism with which he has enriched our sensibility, our imagination and our religiosity.'

In Brazil several great cities jostle for supremacy. But the vast rural areas of Argentina are dominated by just one great city, although 65 per cent of Argentineans live in towns. Buenos Aires, with a population close to nine million stands on the shores of the River Plate. As you stare across its vast expanse of muddy water you might be looking at a European sea.

Buenos Aires has a wide variety of architecture with its fair share of modernity. There are tree-lined streets, the noisy Boca district, the fine shopping centers, the slums, the car-less Florida down which the great crowds walk on weekends and holidays, the many cinemas – a 71

Caracas (Population 2,000,000)

NORTH ATLANTIC OCEAN

VENEZUELA

Georgetown (Population 184,824)

Mackenzie Paramaribo (Population 123,000)
(Population 25,000)

SURINAM Fr. Cayenne (Population 25,700)
GUIANA

COLOMBIA

GUYANA

PERU

R. Amazon

R. Jurua

R. Tapajós

R. Purus

BRAZIL

R. Tocantins

R. S. Francisco

Recife
(Population 1,000,000)

Brasilia (Population 544,800) Salvador

BOLIVIA

PACIFIC

OCEAN

Belo Horizonte (Population 1,200,000)

R. Paraná

PARAGUAY

Rio de Janeiro (Population 4,200,000)

São Paulo (Population 6,000,000)

Asuncion
(Population 300,000)

ARGENTINA

SOUTH ATLANTIC

OCEAN

URUGUAY

Buenos Aires
(Population 2,900,000)
(Suburbs 8,700,000)

Montevideo (Population 1,100,000)

SCALE 0   500   1000 km

0   500   Miles

Mar del Plata

Rio's Ipenema beach – inspiration for a famous lovesong – brings together Brazilians of all colors. But color still counts in Brazil.

European city. The Americans brought in business know-how and although the 'Yanqui imperialism' mood is diminished, Buenos Aireans sometimes look up sardonically at the huge Coca-Cola sign that dominates part of the city. The Buenos Airean is in fact acutely aware of being European. At the same time he is not quite sure that he is as fully European as the first immigrant. As Argentina's greatest writer, Borges, put it, it is like the relationship of some Jews to their countries; they are of their country and yet aware of being both more and less than it. The visit to Europe – to Paris, Rome, Madrid and now to London – has always been an important part of the prosperous Argentine city dweller's education.

The city of Buenos Aires had small beginnings. Once the little riverside town of Puerto de Santa Maria del Buen Aire, it was first established in 1536 – named after either the patron saint of navigators or the fresh breezes of the River Plate. It was later evacuated and moved to its present site; a city founded by ten Spaniards, 50 creoles, 500 cows and 1,000 horses. The British are not aware that they once unsuccessfully invaded Argentina; but the Argentineans remember.

The *invasions inglesas* and their defeat – to be known in the history of Argentina as the *Reconquista* – showed the first signs of Argentine populism. It also launched a long Argentine-Anglo Saxon relationship that varies between friendliness and antagonism to this day. In 1806 the ill-fated British Commodore, Sir Home Popham, occupied Buenos Aires with English and Scots troops. Over a million dollars of prize money was sent to Britain; the booty was paraded through London in eight waggons each drawn by six horses, gay with ribbons and flags on which were inscribed in gold letters the word 'Treasure'. The people of Buenos Aires nevertheless rose against their invaders and won the day.

It was not the last time that street fighting came to Buenos Aires. And, typical of Anglo-Argentine relations, in no time at all English businessmen were back in Argentina. Great Britain helped to develop Argentina's meat trade and has left behind English oases like the Hurlingham Club and the Harrods department store.

The great flow of Italian and Spanish immigrants at the end of the 19th century brought fresh impulses to the older Argentine attitudes. It has today produced a distinctive character that at the same time includes a number of conflicting strands. The urban awareness and the consciousness of European culture do not exclude a strong sense of the Argentine past, a sense of the pampa and its gaucho history. Just as Brazil's heroes are its Bandeirantes, the tenacious settlers who gradually fought their way into the great interior, prospecting and founding settlements in spite of the hostile country, so Argentina celebrates the more flamboyant gauchos.

Gauchos were the lords of the pampas, constantly on the move in search of new pasture for their cattle herds, contemptuous of the city-dwellers, proud of their horse-manship, and unfalteringly loyal to their chosen leaders. Indeed the gaucho idea included the Spanish *hidalgo* concept of nobility. The legendary gaucho friendships are a reality, even among city dwellers. And in many *estancia* restaurants in Buenos Aires a modern decor contrasts with a display of saddles, spurs, bits, horns, *bolas* and other gaucho finery which adorn the walls.

A strong literary and artistic culture has taken root in Buenos Aires. There are art galleries, literary reviews, and a splendid national opera house. A fine literary tradition has flowed from the 'gaucho' writers, and from moderns such as Borges, Casares and Cortazar. Buenos Aires also has a rare appeal for writers, that compares with the appeal of Dublin to James Joyce, London to Dickens, and New York to poets like Whitman and Hart Crane. In the 1920s Buenos Aires was something of a cult with writers. Always conscious of their European cultural heritage, it was as if they were persuading themselves that their roots were here and not in Paris or Rome. 'I have always been (and will be) in Buenos Aires' wrote Borges, who nevertheless, in his seventies, developed a passion for everything Anglo-Saxon.

The most striking popular culture which emerged from Spanish, Italian and French intermingling in Argentina is rather less fierce. It is the tango. In Europe the tango is regarded as one of the more established forms of popular ballroom dancing. In Argentina, and particularly in Buenos Aires, it is an art form. Borges has written lyrics for tangos. And in the 'cathedral of tangos', in Talcahuano y Charcas, they have tango concerts with all the gravity of chamber music concerts. The musicians on the stage look dignified dressed in their dark suits and gleaming shoes. The singer will go through a repertoire of love tangos, sad tangos, criminal tangos, and comic tangos. However, in Buenos Aires international youth culture has drawn young people away from the tango towards modern international pop music.

Argentine attitudes towards *machismo*, the masculine ideals of strength and competition have gone deep. In the Argentine's most popular sport, football, *machismo* is much in evidence. The great stadiums of Buenos Aires testify to its gladiatorial appeal. Argentine football is noted throughout the world for its great skill and some of its finest players go to European clubs. But it is also so notorious for its aggressiveness, that jail sentences have been passed on offenders. So strong are the demands of *machismo* however that punishment has little effect. 'The other man must be pushed a little' is a dictum practised in Argentine football as in other activities. Fights on the football field are not uncommon. Even in the stories of Borges, this most intellectual, eclectic and enigmatic of writers, *machismo* is present in force. He has stories in which a theme is repeated: one man goes out alone, knife in hand, to face the challenge of the other. It is as if Joyce or Yeats had written of boxing. Behind the wheel the citizens of Buenos Aires must rank among the world's most ferociously competitive drivers: 'We drive to scare the soul out of the other man' they say.

The Spanish *caudillo* influence has produced a number of exponents of *caudillismo*, the popular leadership cult. As Americo de Castro has pointed out, the old loyalty to a personal leader which was a characteristic of Spain in the Middle Ages with its frontier battles against the Moors, was transplanted to Latin America. The drive of conquistadors that led them to conquer unknown kingdoms throughout the continent arose, in part, out of loyalty to strong leaders. There was in the early 19th century the tyrannical Juan Manuel Rosas, the idol of the gauchos and the darling of the clergy. And later that century, there was the self-styled schoolmaster president Sarmiento, who combined a belief in popular education with a ruthlessness to other contenders for popular leadership. And there was Perón.

Juan Perón combined *caudillo* appeal with some of the spectacular stage management of Fascism, as well as drawing on familiar Latin syndicalist ideas. His approach was populist and he and his wife Evita left their mark on the working class. His success rebutted the theory that Fascism or neo-Fascism is a middle class phenomenon, resisted by the workers. The continuing Peronist yearnings of many members of the urban working class and trade unions remains an awkward political reality. Argentineans on the whole still believe that charisma is a vital political art.

Argentina has measured itself against Europe and, sometimes uneasily, felt itself lacking; against the United States, and – admiring American know-how, drive and expertise – feared economic domination. It has also measured itself against its neighbor Brazil. In 1864 the jurist Carlos Calvo wrote: 'The Argentine Republic is called upon to be, within a half century, if we have peace, as considerable a power in South America as are the United States in the north, and then will be the moment to settle accounts with that colossus with feet of paper, the Empire of Brazil.' Over fifty years ago, the sociologist, José Ingenieros, asserted *à propos* Brazil; 'the formation of great nations is incompatible with the climatic conditions of the tropics', and incompatible also because of an infusion of negro blood. Since the growth of the great multi-racial Brazilian cities, the European Argentineans are not so sure.

Buenos Aires Stock Exchange, one of the few remaining Spanish colonial buildings, is a major international financial center.

Rio de Janeiro spreads
upwards, with a constantly
increasing congestion — as
these travelers on the
British-built tramways know.

75

As country folk flood the
cities, street photographers
record the newcomers,
in their best Sunday clothes,
for posterity.

Macumba and the Afro-Brazilian cults Brazil

Particularly among Brazil's
negroes, Macumba is strong.
The cults' Angolan roots have
been enriched by Amerindian
and Christian influences.

Already by ten o'clock on the last evening of the year, most people have converged on the beach. Everyone in Rio de Janeiro looks forward to the macumba New Year. Many have been there for hours, preparing their offerings to Iemanjá, Goddess of the Sea.

The entire crescent of the sea-shore is ablaze with the light of candles, and pitted like the surface of an enormous crater. The shore itself is cluttered with massed people and their offerings. Shapes are sculpted in the sand – crosses, five-pointed stars, castle-like mounds or gaping hollows, all covered with candles and flowers. Most flowers are white, symbolizing goodness. Offerings of bottles of cashasa are supplemented by many little gifts to flatter the well-known vanity of the sea-goddess – combs, mirrors, ribbons, perfumes. There are large cloths spread with entire meals of cakes and sweets, together with bottles and glasses of champagne. An old woman, in the customary white embroidered dress and head-scarf, arranges her offering with care and tenderness. She constantly mumbles prayers, and kisses each object before placing it beside the others. The offerings constitute her week's wages. The spirit of giving is unquestioning; the Goddess has her due. The macumba groups are at the heart of the excitement. Their shrines are elaborate and crowded with paintings of the sea-goddess and statues of the Christian saints, variously interpreted. St George conquering the dragon's fire, red to symbolize evil, becomes the god of strength. Each group is led by a *pai y mae de Santos*, father and mother of the Saints. They are all dressed in white, the women in turbans and long dresses, hung with beads. Some leaders wear enormous Indian feather head-dresses. The throb of the drums, which accompany the African chants, is incessant. The air is heavy with incense and strong cheroots.

The rhythms change, and fill the air with a new urgency. The people come impulsively to life. Led by the *mae de Santos*, they are worked to a fever pitch. Consciousness changes to trance. They fling themselves into a frenzy of contorted dancing. Friends guard them from injury. Many rush to the sea to be with their Goddess – and every year a few drown. Some are like puppets whose masters have tangled the strings and try to unravel them by pulling frantically. Each limb is shaken as if it would become detached from the body. Gradually, after such a tremendous physical outburst, they take on the appearance of clockwork dolls running down. Yet still the rhythm pulses on.

Towards dawn, the beach is strewn with sleeping bodies, lying at random where they have been standing till their legs can no longer bear them. A few macumba groups are still active; as light spreads they arouse themselves for a last effort before they disappear into the everyday world. Women go to the sea to wash their colored beads. Silhouetted against the rising sun, with the pink waves playing with their long skirts, they them-

The great annual
Macumba celebration is at
New Year on Rio de Janeiro's
beaches, but there are
cultists in the jungle too.

A woman collapses in a
trance near the gifts that
have been offered to the
Macumba gods. Fellow
cultists stand around in awe.

selves take on the form of the Sea Goddess.

The names of Brazil's famous Afro-Brazilian, or
possession, cults are as stirring as the throb of the ceremonial drums that celebrate them: macumba and umbanda in Rio, batuque in Rio Grande de Sul, candomblé
in Bahia, xango in Pernambuco, pagelance in the
Amazon area. Originally Yoruba or Bantu from Africa,
or Tupi-Guarani Indian, and then colonized by the
Portuguese accent, these names resound with the wealth
of Brazil's folk heritage.

It is mainly from this cultural viewpoint that they are
treated by anthropologists. They solemnly trace some
chosen detail from its African origin and then pronounce
whether the cult in question is 'authentic'. Or else the
cults are described by journalists as fascinating patterns
of folk belief spiced with exotic secrets that only cult-
leaders – and the writer – share. Neither approach does
the cults justice. The first neglects their vitality as state-
ments of life; the second ignores their symbolic, artistic
and philosophical depth. Most observers would compare
the garrulous spirit called Foul Mouth (Boca Suja), for
example, unfavorably with a spirit like Oxala, the
dignified chief of the Yoruba gods; indeed they would
probably dismiss Foul Mouth as an intruder or joke. Yet
for many cult members Foul Mouth is a divinity every
bit as good as the next, even if he is rather unfashionable.
Although he cannot compete with Oxala's connection
with Africa, he and countless colleagues (Sultan of the

Macumba gives a
chance to the poor and the
underdog to break out and
experience an exaltation
that is usually denied.

A store in Rio shows Macumba's versatility: St George is next to Iemanjá, goddess of the sea; beads and pipes surround Jesus.

Woods, Old Black, Martin Fisherman, Cowboy and others) have a good many pertinent comments on contemporary Brazil. Which is what the cults are mostly about.

Brazilian beliefs come from a remarkable range of sources: the shamanism of South American Indians, West African possession cults, European spiritism, Protestantism – particularly of the evangelical variety – and from official and folk Catholicism. All except the official Catholic element, which has the least popular appeal, involve some form of possession.

Anthropologists tend to isolate the various cults and, referring to them as fading 'cultural survivals' from a mainly African past, turn them into fossils. In fact the cults are living complexes of religious and social behavior, valued by an already vast and growing number of Brazilians who are neither exclusively nor even predominantly rustic or non-European. It is as difficult to establish their numbers as it is to establish their identity. However the participants do tend to be notably female and, with exceptions, they are mostly poor. Africans, Indians and Europeans are not, except in history, distinct groups in Brazil. Brazilian society is now based on class rather than on ethnic origins. Cults of different ethnic origins have, like the different peoples of Brazil, become gradually mingled. It is as difficult and unrealistic to sort the cults into types as it is to make and evaluate distinctions between their members.

Some cults, however, are less mixed, their ethnic origins more evident, than others. There are candomblés in Bahia, for example, which still use exclusively African and especially Yoruba languages and drum rhythms. But none of the cults have entirely escaped the influence of others. Macumba and umbanda especially are combined products; their followers possessed simultaneously by Indios, caboclos, African orixas, folk Catholic saints and figures straight from spiritism, like the Pretos Velhos – or Old Blacks – the souls of slaves who received no proper burial.

The participants in macumba, candomblé and xango and the rest, although aware of distinctions between them, see the cults as basically linked. All the cults exchange rituals and beliefs, and share several fundamental features. Every cult follower belongs to a cult house under a priest or priestess, usually called 'father' – or 'mother' – of the saints. Every member is formally initiated, and associated with either one specific divinity, usually known as a saint, or with a series of them. Every member is, above all, possessed by the saints in elaborate ceremonies in the cult house or in other spots associated with the saint, accompanied by drums, songs, mutual compliments and feasts.

The best known ceremony is possibly that of Iemanjá, which well illustrates the eclecticism of many of the cults. Imanjá, the sea goddess, is derived from many sources. Her origin is partly Orixa (a West African divinity); partly the wayward water-spirit of Indian mythology –

As the dawn of New Year breaks on Rio's Copacabana Beach, cultists cluster round gifts to Iemanjá, vain goddess of the sea.

A woman's trance carries her into a world of her own, as she sings chants that reveal the hybrid pagan and Christian nature of Macumba.

A follower of the Macumba sea goddess takes offerings out to sea. If washed up, she has rejected them; if swept out to sea, they are accepted.

her macumba title is 'mother of the water'; and partly mermaid – a favorite character in the songs of lonely Portuguese sailors in Brazil. Her followers tend not to be conscious of these distinctions in her origin although they do have varied images of her, which incorporate a number of human qualities.

The cults reveal aspects of Brazil's kaleidoscopic social history which would otherwise have faded into obscurity. In Bahia, for instance, the candomblés of 'Brazilian' saints are the Bantu ones from Angola rather than the Yoruba ones. Even for their African orixas, the Bahians use caboclo music in an intimacy with Indian cults. This came about because, although most of the field-slaves on the sugar plantations were of Bantu origin, when they escaped they came into contact with Indians and caboclos – the half-Indian, half Portuguese peasants of the backlands. The connection with the caboclos is frowned on by the more conservative of the 'African' disciples.

Brazil's different regions are physically isolated, but its poor have always been on the move: fleeing from slavery and droughts, or searching for employment, from the Amazon rubber boom to São Paulo's industries or the new capital of Brasilia. As they wandered, their culture and blood became mixed and they merged into a varied but single class. The cults are their class religion. Class gives the cults coherence.

81

Macumba Brazil

The New Year sun rises. A
woman cultist purifies
herself by washing her beads
in the sea, before
returning to the slums.

A dead Macumba follower,
covered with a newspaper,
is protected from
evil spirits by candles
offered by colleagues.

This accounts for the way people join them. Urban poverty produces a feeling of alienation, especially among women, who bear the heavier burdens. To 'have a saint', who sings and dances in the guise of a god, reverses cruel reality. Membership is not hereditary, but can be gained by attending ceremonies, or else through full-scale initiation and daily ritual duties. Cult houses are usually in poor areas (favelas, for instance) or in secret places just outside the town. People are often drawn into a cult through a visit to a cult house to 'consult the saint' of the priest or priestess over some personal problem. Their problems are usually problems of poverty: the lack of a house or job, or an illness which is too expensive to cure. They often say they were drawn into it by an involuntary possession that indicated an obligation to the saint. This however usually coincides with the strain of some personal crisis.

Cults reassert the value of the undervalued: the individual, reduced to anonymity by poverty, is almost rebuilt by the experience of possession. He feels rehabilitated. Possession is at first violent, but becomes calm as the saint is tamed and the person is healed – although the epidemic (the state of society itself) continues. The priest or priestess is like a favorite neighbor, doctor, psychiatrist and parent – all rolled into one. Suicide tendencies are interpreted as signs of the saint's annoyance at neglect rather than misery from social oppression. The cult returns to its members a sense of identity which society has plundered. Certainly cult-members do have a self-assurance and strength of personality that is rare at their level of society.

The Indians and caboclos are people at the butt-end of society, hunted and starved, quintessences of under-privilege. Cult members look up not only to their saints but also to each other. The cults give them confidence. In the cult house – even if they are only there on a casual visit – and in the cult ceremonies with their elaborate greetings to the saints the poor become gods. In the cult houses they see enacted their own unwritten history. The self-esteem which ritual returns to the oppressed is also restored through the mythology of the cults. Their songs tell of wattle and daub houses, hunger and difficulties as well as happiness and freedom.

Once for an entire night I watched a favorite caboclo, Martin the Fisherman, enact his myths. These asserted the divinity in man's frailty: though crushed, man was capable of nobility and vision; he was tragic, yet comic. I was reminded of King Lear.

Where there is authoritarianism in society, in the cults there is egalitarianism. In the cults community feeling overwhelms individual striving. And the participant experiences things for himself, instead of having experience inflicted upon him. This is especially true of women. The family, like the patriarchal society of which it is the fundamental unit, is male-dominated. It is the unique social privilege of the poor man to dominate his family. The result for his wife is that under-privilege is brought into the home. Her under-privileged position is reversed in the cult ritual, especially when it is conducted by a priestess. In the rituals women are possessed by saints – who are usually male – and, mocking virility and the myths which sustain male dominance, they settle their scores with the male spectators. The speciality of the cult of Foul Mouth, for example, is to scorn romantic love with earthy cynicism. It is particularly popular with women. The cults give women a unique chance to break out against domestic repression. In many households it is enough to deflate a domineering husband, just to threaten to leave home and go and live in a cult house. Some women are as good as their word.

Long ago, although the Brazilian authorities try to hide it, candomblés were a source of slave revolts. The authorities highlight the purely 'African' cults, emphasizing their glamor and the excitement of their dancing, without looking at who takes part in them, and why. The cults are indeed exotic and spectacular. They are also a unique way of confronting and overcoming human problems.

83

With the help of a priest-confessor, cultists' sins are forgiven. They yelp in imitation of dogs, to signify their expiation.

The white élite
Lowland South America

The fortunes of the great old aristocratic families of Brazil have risen and fallen in almost exact harmony with those of the great sugar and coffee plantations on which their prosperity was based. 'Rapid rise, passing glory, and irreversible decay' is how Josué de Castro, one of Brazilian society's most perceptive observers, described the history of the plantations in the northeastern coastlands. So it is with the social history of Brazil, itself largely the story of coffee and sugar: its production, successful at first, then its decline, and its devastation throughout of man and animal alike.

It was a devastation which profoundly affected, yet did not destroy, the aristocratic families. In industry, politics and in economic life, the old families still have power and influence. Nevertheless the 'first families' of Brazil today are not the same as the plantation families of the 18th and 19th centuries. Time and economic change have reshaped the patriarchal family of the aristocrat into something anthropologists would call a kindred. Brazilians call it a parentela. Comparable patterns exist in Brazil's neighbors – Argentina and Chile, and indeed in Peru, Colombia and Venezuela. Even those non-Lusitanian, post-colonial families of southern Brazil and Argentina – many of them with Italian or British origins – who have become great landowners, as breeders of cattle and horses, have evolved the same kind of widely ramified family networks.

A member of a parentela, such as the aristocratic Brazilian family, regards all his relations, including those of marriage on both his mother's and father's side, as his kinsmen; he even has ties with the god-parents of all these relatives. All these people are in a sense his family. He can call upon the support of dozens, possibly hundreds of people, with whom he shares a memory of a common past. The members of an aristocratic parentela can claim connections with a history that goes back to the 1750s, a common struggle from then until the present day for possessions, prosperity, position and power against a backdrop of constant economic and social uncertainty. Today they share fears and hopes for the future.

By the end of the 18th century the great plantations stretched from Para in the north through to the northeast, to the lowland valleys of Rio de Janeiro. There were vast tracts of available land, an influx of negro slaves from Angola and Mozambique and government capital and expertise were at the developers' disposal. And there was an upsurge in the demand for Brazilian products abroad. All this encouraged the plantations of sugar, coffee, cotton, cocoa, indigo and rice.

It was a boom that in 1780 nobody could have predicted. Nobody expected the demand for Brazilian sugar, cotton, or coffee to expand; for events like the slave revolution in Haiti (Sainte Domingue), and the Napoleonic wars and their attendant effects on Europe's markets and overseas suppliers were entirely fortuitous. Most of the families who found themselves riding high

The fortunes of many of the old landed families are as high as ever. The *hacienda* stretches for miles. The mansion is fit for a prince.

The élite of South America
has kept up a benevolent
paternalism, breeding cattle
and horses, and dipping into
the ever-changing politics.

on the boom tide of those years were conscious that
demand for their products rested on fortuitious, unfore-
seen and therefore unstable factors, and that their
fortunes could as easily vanish.

Yet for the plantation owner his wealth was hard won.
He had to invest heavily in land and labor. As sugar
cane took some 13 to 18 months to mature, land would
be tied up in production for long periods, so he needed
a great deal of land. He also needed a great number of
men to weed the crop, and clear and burn new ground,
and he had to buy slaves at great cost from coastal
traders. All this investment in land and slaves would
yield relatively little unless the planter could secure the
use of a mill for grinding the cane and separating the
sugar from molasses. For work in the mill more slaves
were needed, and technical staff to supervize them.

It was to his family that the patriarchal plantation
owner looked to maximize his control over his land,
beasts and labor. The owner was effectively the legal
and spiritual head of his entire family. He ruled it
autocratically. Women, sons and daughters were all
subject to his domination. They asked for his blessing.
And they bowed to his will. Marriages were arranged
with a view to extending or cementing family ties. At
the beginning of the 19th century marriages were usually
arranged between young 13 or 14 year old girls and very
much older men. Further family links would be established when children were baptized. The godfather – the
padrinho – and godmother were responsible for the
child's spiritual and temporal education. The position of
padrinho, especially, was one of great honor, and some
power, since it entitled him to unrestricted access to his
a filhado and thus to the child's entire household.

According to the inheritance laws of Brazil, when the
plantation owner died his landholding had to be divided
between his heirs. Most families during this period had
eight to ten children and plantations could rapidly be
broken up on the death of the owners. It was the aim of
every plantation owner during his lifetime to allocate
his lands to his sons and daughters in such a way that
they would remain firmly linked and *fazendas* and mills
would continue to be worked together without disruption.
Owners would distribute their great blocks of land
among their sons, who would be married to the daughters
of neighboring landowners. And they would give their
daughters land as dowries on their marriages to their
neighbors' sons. Grandchildren would be made *afilhados*
of their grandfathers and uncles. At every stage families,
and their interests, would be consolidated.

In the great houses of the plantation owners, the
children's education was constantly and closely super-
vized. Little boys would be taught by tutors at home and
would already by the age of six or seven assume the air
and authority of *senhores* or little masters. A little girl
would be surrounded by bevies of maiden aunts, negro
house slaves and servants and carefully reared on gossip

The well-to-do of 'good' families in Buenos Aires gather at the Hurlingham Club, founded by the English, for polo or a rubber of bridge.

and incessant intrigue all of which would be indispensible later when she became mistress of her own great house.

By the 1850s many sons were being brought up in the expectation that their future would be outside the plantation. The successful plantation owner increasingly had to promote his interests beyond his own property as the economic power of the central government expanded and spread. It was in the 1850s that the plantation owners began to build their splendid town houses in Rio de Janeiro, the capital. In these houses they could instal their sons, so that they could secure places in local government and vast credits to build railroads and steamship lines to carry sugar and cotton across the entire country and to overseas markets.

The scene for matchmaking moved increasingly from the great halls of the plantation mansions to the drawing rooms and studies of the smart new town houses. In this new setting marriages could now be transacted at a national level. A son's student friends from the Medical School or the Law School would be invited to listen to the lovely but maidenly daughter of the house play the piano. The gentlemen, resplendently dressed in the latest male fashion, would be presented with a fine cigar, as mother, daughters and maiden aunts bustled round them dressed in the approved incongruously austere finery.

The power and prestige of the parentela began to range over great distances as planters' sons married Rio bankers' daughters, and planters' daughters married the sons of judges, lawyers and doctors. Families acquired *padrinhos* in ever-widening circles and ever-different professional and economic milieux. Soon the son of the planter was in intimate contact with everybody who could conceivably and legitimately help him run his business. The government itself became the business of the plantation. Nevertheless it was in this period that the patriarch planter's power began to erode as his sons and political colleagues would gather in groups, known as chapels, within the parentela.

Today members of the parentela keep contact with even their most far-flung kinsmen by automobile and airplane, both of which are well within their resources. Far from being superseded by the new technology they have made even this serve their interest, enabling them to take a full and mobile role in government as well as in business. Positions in the government, awarded for past favors, are the reward for many members of a parentela. They have now become one of the most important bastions of the parentela and enable its members to promote and protect their income.

The parentela has come to town.

87

Vaqueiros
Brazil

On an afternoon in late May 1927 the vaqueiro Ze Teixeira drove the cattle herd of Cerqueira Bulcao up into the cool pastures of the Serra dos Gerais away from the graying scrub and sun-blistered lands of the valley of the São Francisco. The cattle had been on the move since dawn. Ze Teixeira had forced his drivers to break camp to get them as fast as possible onto the upper slopes of the Serra dos Gerais. Urged on by the scent of better lands, the cattle and horses appeared to possess new energy; they ceased the monotonous shambling which had marked their long trail from the *fazendas* – cattle ranches – on the confluence of the Rio São Francisco and the Rio Grande.

Up in the serra, away from the drought-stricken lowlands, the scrawny cattle could fatten up in time to be taken down onto the plains by September. Here, in the deserted range of plateaux that runs across the center of Brazil, the cattle would run free, identifiable only by the brand of Cerqueira Bulcao's *fazenda*. They were all vulnerable to the ravages both of marauding Indians and of jaguars.

The vaqueiro, the Brazilian cowboy, today is regarded as the authentic Brazilian: independent, proud and immune to pressure; free from the talons either of landowners or of foreign traders. Here was a man who appeared to live close to the soil of Brazil, garnering food from the interior of the sub-continent. Here was a man whose very livelihood, whether hunting or being hunted, depended upon his wits. This romantic perception of the vaqueiro attracts both the realist and the nationalist in Brazilian society. A figure from the past, the vaqueiro appeals to the sentiments of those who feel the artificiality of city life, who find its ostentation irksome, who resent citified un-Brazilian habits. Such men revel in the 'catch, kill and eat' philosophy of the vaqueiro.

The vaqueiro's simple ways, his independent life and his direct, if unsubtle, humor transcend barriers of class or race within Brazilian society. In whisky-clouded gatherings, in banter at a liquor stall manned by some corpulent Portuguese, the vaqueiro and his doings are a constant source of conversation. And yet his activities as a cattleman have long ceased to be of great importance to the vast majority of the population, even in the northeast of Brazil.

In retrospect the early 18th century must have appeared as something of a golden age for the vaqueiros. The lands were open, and the range was good. The period of great droughts had not set in and forest cover was thick. The vaqueiro clothed himself in deerskin from head to foot, rode high in the saddle across vast regions, oblivious to demands of time and money. He watched the herds of the great *fazendas* multiply under his gaze and to his own advantage.

Historians have talked of the vaqueiros living in a world of leather. Leather hats, jackets, chaps and leggings protected him against the rigors of the heat,

89

Vaqueiros — cowboys — are
white, Indian, or the sons of
black slaves; all are proudly
committed to their 'catch,
kill and eat' philosophy.

against the vicious spears of cacti, against animals and even against the Indian arrows. Leather flaps served as doors and window shutters on the baked mud and wood walls of his hut on the *fazenda*; leather buckets held manioc flour and water, grain and tobacco; leather made ties for his *charque* (sun-dried meat) and sheaths for his long dagger or trusty musket. The vaqueiro seemed almost self-sufficient. He needed money only for powder, tobacco, guns and sometimes salt.

It was with an air of independence, of certain and secure knowledge of the world around him, the tricks of his trade, and above all the moods of cattle, that Ze Teixeira in 1927 jostled the herd, his drovers and their inseparable dogs towards the winter pastures of the Serra dos Gerais. His short figure, prematurely wizened face, slow speech and deceptively slow gait, spoke of a man aware of himself and his standing in society. His rugged independence had been won in direct confrontation with the rigors and natural might of the country of the *Sertão*, the inhospitable backlands of central and northern Brazil.

The system of open-range extensive cattle ranching, dominated by the *fazenda*-owner, the *proprietario*, and his faithful vaqueiros, demanded vast quantities of land. In the São Francisco valley each head of cattle needed at least 15 acres to survive. Further to the north and west each cow needed more than 25 acres. Cattle were valuable, land was not. Men such as Cerqueira Bulcao, who owned herds of over seven hundred head needed upwards of 25,000 acres on which to raise them. In the winter months, they needed further access to large areas of free range on the serras or Chapada mountains to provide cool pastures and relief from the drought.

By the early 18th century *proprietarios*, the fore-runners of men such as Cerqueira Bulcao, could maintain their grazing rights over the land through their influence at the colonial capital, Salvador da Bahia. Governors of the city were aware not only of the territorial influence of the *proprietarios* in the *Sertão*, but also of the relative impotence of government. They were quick to grant land to men who could guarantee both order in the interior and the vital cattle supplies for the coastal sugar and tobacco plantations and for the dangerously hungry city itself. Ranchers like Cerqueira Bulcao, the Pires de Carvalho e Albuquerque and other families had long used their influence with the Portuguese governors to gain land sufficient for vaqueiros like Ze Teixeira to raise cattle.

Except for river boundaries, *proprietarios* and vaqueiros tended neither to know nor to worry about the limits of their lands. In the *Sertão* it was the bulls and their attendant cows, not men and fences, which determined boundaries. Only the few subsistence crops such as manioc and beans grown around the corral were fenced against the cattle. The vaqueiro tended his herds as they moved, especially in the winter pastures of the Gerais or

The 'age of leather' is not over in north-east Brazil, where vaqueiros drive their zebu cattle to market across mile upon mile of dry *sertão*.

(Below) The vaqueiro's simple, hardy, frontiersman's life has long possessed a mystical appeal for Brazil's innumerable city-dwellers.

90

Skill with the lasso dates back three centuries. It is required as much today as ever for the round-up of the steers.

the Chapada.

In the summer, from October onwards to March of the following year, the rains would come to the parched scrublands of the *Sertão*. The desert suddenly took on a verdant bloom. Cattle which were fierce in the dry season could be tamed and even milked; herds could be rounded up; horses could be broken in. Milking, rounding up and breaking his horses, the vaqueiro was proud master of the *fazenda*, performing in the corral with a vigor and verve unexpected of the man who seemed to shamble along in the droughts of May or June.

In October the *proprietario* arrived from Salvador or one of the other commercial centres of the *Sertão*. Drovers and teams of oxen were hired: cattle were rounded up and branded. At round-up the *proprietario* divided the ownership of the calves and yearlings among his vaqueiros, each was allowed a quarter of the new-born animals. The vaqueiros like Ze Teixeira regarded the allocation not merely as payment for services but also as a recognition of their value as men. It was a measure of their honor and their prowess with man and beast alike. It was an act of trust as well as a commercial contrast between *proprietario* and vaqueiro, a homage

to both men. The casting of lots, a practice among equals, was the recognition of their agreement, a relationship between men who understood each other.

The understanding between vaqueiro and *proprietario* was further cemented by the fact that the vaqueiro's cattle were reared and sent to market alongside the cattle of his owner. This arrangement was to everyone's advantage. There were long distances involved in cattle rearing and this demonstrated the visible understanding or contract between *proprietario* and vaqueiros. The vaqueiros would care for all cattle equally, since the size of his payment depended directly upon the largest possible output of calves and yearlings. On his part, the *proprietario* would see to it that his herds won a good price and received good pastures in the long drive across north-eastern Brazil to the coastal markets.

The spread of this system of cattle culture grew up through the 16th and mid-17th centuries primarily in response to the growth of the sugar plantations on the north-east coast of Brazil. The independence of the vaqueiro and the social standing of the *proprietario* were then part of a vast pattern of trade in sugar, cattle, slaves and foodstuffs, involving towns the world over: 91

Vaqueiros wear open sandals
with spurs when it is too
hot to wear boots. Droughts
may last for months at a
time and cattle must be moved.

Mozambique, Buenos Aires, Potosi, Maranhao, London, Lisbon and Naples. In a world dominated by sugar and slaves the vaqueiro appeared as the only man who possessed some assurance of prosperity and improvement through his work. The division of new-born calves assured him of a chance to win ownership of a new herd which he might then pasture with that of his *proprietario*. Since land was both unmarked and readily available, the vaqueiro could become a *proprietario;* a man who might then enjoy the privilege and honor due to a *hidalgo* nobleman.

This ambition of equality with the *proprietario* gave the vaqueiro the economic backbone to his honor and bearing. The vaqueiro possessed security of tenure in his relationship with the *proprietario,* and travelers noted his evident pride in the maintenance of the *fazenda*. The vaqueiro took pride in his horses and the care taken in the planting of the *rocas* which produced his food. His was a unique position within the Brazilian society of the 17th century. For the vaqueiros, it was a golden age.

The conditions that allowed the vaqueiro his independence were the vast stretches of virtually uninhabited and undisputed summer and winter pastures. Here were open pastures in which the cattle could herd naturally around the young and old bulls; free inter-breeding; absolute primacy of land-use for the open range; long slow access to markets which were quite unconcerned with the quality of the beef produced; and the existing government which was, to say the least, physically and socially remote from the regions in which cattle were raised.

These conditions still persist in certain areas of north-eastern and central Brazil today; in parts of Piaui, Rio Grande do Norte, Western Bahia and Goiás. In these areas the owners still divide new-born calves with the vaqueiros, proud figures astride their horses at the market-place and the cattle-fair. The age of leather is not yet over. But these areas, which lie hundreds of miles north of Brasilia, thousands of miles west of Bahia and Recife, are shrinking. They are no longer unin-habited, nor given over entirely to cattle. They are opened up by the new roadways to the south.

Elsewhere, across the vast regions of the north-east, the independent vaqueiro becomes a historical character for the novelist. He has been slowly yet irrevocably eased out by the collapse of the conditions which made possible the *fazendas* and the dividing of calves. Towards the end of the 18th century the mining activities at the head-waters of many of the great rivers of the north-east were already destroying the ecological balance so necessary to the regularity of the river courses. In other areas, overgrazing, encouraged by the mining regions' demand for meat, denuded vast regions of the country. Rivers flowed more irregularly than before, wrecking banks and flooding large areas, or disappearing altogether. Droughts lasted longer. Rains did not always appear. Cattle died in their thousands and tens of thousands. The drought became more widespread, and this is a process which is still going on. All this increased the pressure of work on the vaqueiro and diminished his chances of a good share out.

Droughts were further encouraged by the spread of cotton planting into the high *Sertão*. From the last quarter of the 18th century to the present day, a combination of ready markets and easy cultivation have made cotton a favored and profitable crop. Gradually and inexorably the Chapadas of the north-east became occupied by men who either owned or rented small areas of lands from the *proprietario*. These men cultivated during the months when the cattle were on the plain; the stubble of their crops was used by the animals of the *proprietario*. The days of unfenced lands were over and *proprietarios* were as concerned with the production of cotton as they had been with cattle. Later they became interested in the production of coffee, sugar, and wax. Gradually the range of the cattleman was reduced.

Already, at the end of the 18th century, in the upper parts of the valley of the São Francisco around Paracatu in Minas Gerais, the growing demand for meat in nearby mining regions and the coastal towns like Rio de Janeiro, were bringing great changes in the world of the vaqueiro. In this region travelers noted that cattle were reared rather more carefully and scientifically than elsewhere; fences were used more frequently and more care was taken in the herding of cattle. Instead of hunting down the cattle, men used the lasso, made from thongs of hide. Bulls were tethered, not allowed to build up their individual harems.

The milking season was longer, and the products of the dairy, traditionally assigned to the vaqueiro for his own use or to sell, were now appropriated and traded by the *proprietario* as cheeses. Boundaries were fixed not by the meanderings of cattle, which formed their own patterns, but by other factors. Gradually *proprietarios*

A vaqueiro keeps his herd
in order with whip and voice
at a *feria* or cattle market —
a rare occasion to
drink and exchange news.

began to pay the vaqueiro for his part of the share-out, a practice which is still widespread today. The aura of understanding and trust, so essential to the physical and social well-being of the vaqueiro, was already beginning to break down.

Further pressures increased the pre-eminence of the *proprietario*. One of them was the simple pressure of population. In a region such as the high *Sertão*, droughts and irregular river courses allow only a small population. As miners and farmers moved into the region, the vaqueiro, and his cattle, came under greater pressure. The vaqueiro was forced to rely more and more upon the political skill and wealth of his protector, the *proprietario*, who was now deeply involved in marketing cotton, carnauba, sugar and coffee. The vaqueiro rapidly became the armed retainer of the *proprietario*, prompt to demonstrate his prowess not against the leopard, but against neighboring landlords.

Throughout the 18th and 19th centuries the *Sertão* of the north-east witnessed the steady encroachment of something resembling government. The liquidation of the Jesuits and their villages provided a spring-board which government officials from Portugal used as a means to extend their influence. They applied ruthless

pressure upon *proprietarios* for the control of their lands and taxation of their herds. The policy of divide and rule fostered by a succession of governments operating from Rio de Janeiro and Bahia forced the independent vaqueiro into conflict with his *proprietario* who was in turn engaged in perpetual feuds with neighboring landowners.

These rivalries forced the vaqueiro to realize the political and military prowess of the *proprietario*. The growth in military power based overwhelmingly in the market towns of the *Sertão* reinforced the pressures of the market place which were inexorably reducing the independence of the vaqueiro, and converting the *proprietario* into a merchant and money lender. The repeating rifle, the railroad and the machine gun served then as the cutting edge of commercial and demographic pressures making continuation of the share out of new-born calves, and all that it implied, precarious indeed.

The great enemy of the independent vaqueiro was a combination of all these things: the prod of a growing population, the more frequent drought, the onslaught of groves of wax-palms and the gradual change that came over his relationship with his *proprietario*. Then a

93

Vaqueiros Brazil

A steer is rudely hauled
aboard a boat bound for
Marajo island at the mouth of
the Amazon, where the
pastures are rich.

new breed of cattle was introduced. And with these cattle came barbed wire fences and the gradual abandoning of free ranges.

The traditional cattle of the *Sertão*, the criollo breed of longhorn first imported by the Spaniards and Portuguese in the 16th century, were famous for their tough hides and ability to withstand the severest droughts. So long as men would eat the sun-dried beef, and find use for their low-quality hides, then the ways of the cattlemen might still be preserved. By the end of the 19th century, however, *proprietarios* in some of the more favoured positions of the borderlands between the *Sertão* and the coastal regions of the Agreste, the fertile uplands, and also in Goias and Minas Gerais realized that the demands of the beef market in Brazil were changing rapidly. The coastal city populations were hungry for fresh meat. And cattle were no longer extensively used as a means of transport.

The 1880s saw the introduction of Indian Zebu cattle. They were far better able to withstand the climate of the north-east, even in times of drought. Zebu were valuable, and *proprietarios* took care to use the new barbed wire to fence off the best lands of the summer pastures. Farmers were encouraged to cultivate bottom lands and Chapada mountain slopes for winter forage. To the *proprietario* the dividing of new-born calves with the vaqueiros ceased to be useful. He wanted to own his entire herd; to isolate his bulls, and to break up the pastures so that he possessed strips of good grassland at any time of year

The advent of more efficient government and access to credit facilities provided the *proprietario* with both money and political support. With these he battered his neighbors into acceptance of barbed wire boundaries and pedigree stock. In these circumstances all the *proprietario* required were tenant farmers and foremen, who would be allowed to cultivate strips of bottom land for three days a week, working the other four for the *proprietario*. Such a system of labor was the enemy of the independent free-ranging life of the vaqueiro.

The coming of the Zebu cattle also spelt the beginning of the end for the great drives which characterized the life of the vaqueiro. In the dawn of the cattle ranges, huge distances had been covered by the hardy criollo cattle, which walked hundreds of miles from the winter pastures to the *fazendas,* to the markets and abattoirs in Recife or Salvador. The lean cattle were fattened in market towns, in places such as Jacobina and Bahia, or Bom Jardim in Pernambuco. Driving cattle over such immense distances, preserving the herd intact was a task that required great skill, for which the vaqueiros were vital. But at market, the cattle only produced a stringy beef. The Zebu cattle, better beef-producers, were sold to more discriminating markets. They were transported by rail or even by truck.

To talk about the traditional vaqueiro is to talk of a 95

Vaqueiros Brazil

Water buffalo drag a canoe-like sledge through the swamps of Murajo to the cattle boat which will be unloading stores, too.

man and a way of life which is now confined to a relatively small area of the Brazilian sub-continent. The conditions which supported the traditional vaqueiro have almost disappeared. Gone are the vast stretches of open, undisputed lands for summer and winter pasture; breeding is controlled to maintain pedigrees and improve quality; the open range is no longer given first to the cattle, for farming has taken hold. Access to markets on the coast and in the south is improving steadily as the years go by. Discriminating export markets for Brazilian meat make *proprietarios* concerned with the quality of their herds; government is ever more pervasive and far more efficient. These things may take away his livelihood, even some of his independence, but they can never take away the pride of the vaqueiro.

Most of all, however, these things do not touch the legend of the vaqueiro, the aura that surrounds his way of life and the man himself. In the dry, burning *Sertão*, he defied the elements and drove the cattle from places where little can survive. His world was the free range; he was a free man. In Brazil, where distances are so vast, he was the restless pioneer who always lived at the edge of civilization. The legend runs deep. It is a legend that still lives in some parts, but also a legend without which many Brazilians would feel sadly removed from the spirit of their country.

96

Many vaqueiros saddled longhorns instead of horses on Marajo. They are better suited to the waterlogged pastures.

At the Santana *feria* in
north-east Brazil, a meat
packing station sells surplus
offal freshly cooked like
hot-dogs.

Jangada fishermen
Brazil

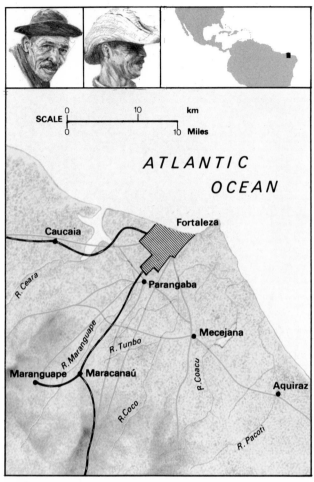

They return, perhaps, in the evening. Across the breakers on the horizon, one by one, the triangular lateen sails draw nearer, pitching and swinging, worked efficiently by men with steering-oars and poles. No hulls are visible, and it seems as if unsupported tangles of sails and men – and nothing else at all – are blowing inland on the swell of the sea, driven by the evening's on-shore breeze. Then as a rolling wave lifts the leading raft its shape is suddenly clear.

Many people crowd together on the beach to see the *jangadas* return: the sons and wives of the *jangadeiros*; the vendors who will buy their catch for marketing inland, a few beggars who hope to earn a fish or two by helping to beach the returning rafts.

Excitement rises as the leading *jangada* plunges across the first of the shore breakers. At once a large stone sheet-anchor is dropped, the raft slews round into the wind, and the four men on board lower the sail and start to pole furiously until – very smoothly and under perfect control – the *jangada* hits the beach. The crew leaps off; they are joined by men and boys from the shore, and the heavy task of beaching the *jangada* begins.

Only when it is some way up the shore, beyond the

The *jangada* balsa log raft,
powered by lateen sails and
steered by oars and poles, is
one of the world's most
primitive sea-going craft.

reach of the highest tides, can the men relax. The sail is re-hoisted to dry, and then the catch is examined, weighed and distributed according to complex local rules. One share goes to the crew, a larger one to the captain; they are always paid in kind, and will take some fish home for their families and sell the rest independently for cash. But the bulk of the catch belongs to the owner of the *jangada*. In the old days, the captain and the owner were one and the same, but now the owner seldom steers his own raft.

It is a picturesque scene; and any observer who sees the *jangadas* coming home, or who watches them at work from the deck of a passing ship, might think romantically about a life so elemental, so dependent on courage and skill, so well-adapted, so stable. He will certainly expose a lot of film and take home some decorative photographs; and if he is bold, he will venture out to sea in a *jangada* and will find it a wildly exciting experience. Once more in his city office, he may sigh wistfully, wishing that he too could be a *jangadeiro*.

He will be right about the courage and skill which this life demands, and right too in a way about its stability. He has witnessed a pattern of life and work that has changed little over the centuries. The *jangada* or log raft is one of the most ancient, primitive sea-going craft in use today. When the Portuguese first explored this north-eastern coast of Brazil in the early 16th century, the Indians were already using the log rafts for fishing; and all along this coast from Fortaleza down to Salvador or Bahia in the south, men still fish with hook and line from *jangadas*. The only addition to the original Indian-designed raft is the sail.

The coastal villagers of north-eastern Brazil are people of mixed, and often largely African, origin whose ancestors were brought here chiefly to work the inland sugar plantations after the local Indians – as elsewhere in South America and the Caribbean – had proved unsuitable for slavery. The Portuguese encouraged the Africans to take over the already established practice of fishing rafts. For the Indians – and with them the *jangadas* – were dying out.

The colonists contributed a sail of Mediterranean

Fishing with handlines,
jangadeiros fill the pot.
But only farmers of plantain
can save enough money for
a net – which means profit.

design, and extended the scope of *jangada* fishing. They also took legal and economic control, so that the fishermen ceased to work for local subsistence only, and became part of the inland economy, supplying food for the plantation hinterland and the towns. It became the prime concern of the men in power to maintain that supply while keeping prices low. As a result the *jangadeiros* do not live in idyllic peasant freedom; their lives and work are complicated by restrictions enforced in other people's interests and their earnings limited by control on the price of fish.

The *jangadas* today are remarkable craft; at sea, they seem so improvised and precarious that their strength can be underestimated. An American sea-captain on his way to Rio de Janeiro, so the story goes, once saw a crude, apparently ramshackle raft far out at sea, with men standing on it, waving frantically. He thought they must be survivors from a shipwreck, and brought his ship closer. But the men were *jangadeiros*, not signalling for help, but touting for custom in the knowledge that they could get a better price for their fresh fish from the ship's captain than from the traders on shore.

For all its apparent crudity, the *jangada* is extraordinarily well adapted for its purpose. It is easy and cheap to make. No metal is used in its construction since rust would cause rotting. The *jangada* is made entirely from wood and vegetable fibers. The basic structure is of logs, perhaps twenty feet long and eight in number, laid side by side and fastened together with long wooden pegs. Only simple tools are used but the *pau de jangada* – the variety of balsa wood from which it is made – is soft, and the *jangadeiros*, who make their own boats, find the wood easy to work. The wooden mast is stepped well forward, and carries a triangular lateen sail: a centerboard keel is lowered for sailing and raised for beaching; there is a wooden bench in the stern for the helmsman, who uses an oar in place of a rudder. Amidships is a small wooden platform where fish are salted and stored, and beneath this a basket in which the fish is kept fresh by the continual flow of the sea-water over the logs: a forked pole is mounted above this, hung with fishing lines, baskets for hooks and bait, and gourds for food and water.

The *paquete* is similar to the *jangada de alto* but smaller: it is made from only six logs some twenty feet long, and usually keeps to in-shore waters. The third and smallest type is the one-man *bote*, made from only four logs and ten to thirteen feet long; it is equipped with a basket, a forked staff, an anchor, and a bench, and no sensible sailor in a *bote* would dare to venture far from land. When it carries a small sail it is known as a *bote a velha*; otherwise it is a *bote de remo*, driven by oars and hardly differing at all from the original Indian log rafts, discovered and renamed by the Portuguese.

The *jangadas* are remarkably stable in a high sea – far more speedy and manoeuvrable than their appearance

Jangada fishermen Brazil

The *jangadeiros'* ancestors were African slaves brought to work on sugar plantations. The Portuguese encouraged them to adopt local Indians' rafts.

The rafts rot and are hard to replace from the dwindling coastal supply of balsa; many *jangadeiros* end up working for wages on sailing boats.

might suggest – and since they draw little water, they can sail over the submerged reefs that abound in these waters and frequently give unwary visiting sailors a nasty surprise. On the other hand the light porous wood, a variety of balsa called *pau de jangada*, from which the boats are made easily becomes waterlogged and has to be dried out scrupulously after use. Even so, the wood progressively deteriorates and rots. It has to be replaced after a year, or at the most every two years. And the *jangada* offers little comfort to its crew. The visitors who will certainly enjoy a brief ride in this unfamiliar craft would not relish a life lived endlessly at sea on one of these. The *jangadeiros* ride on a permanently waterlogged raft for perhaps two

days at a time, with no protection either from the blistering sea or from the icy gales, usually soaked from head to foot, and never entirely safe.

The larger *jangadas* are very sturdy, almost ocean-worthy craft. Mestre Geronimo, a famous raftsman who was lost at sea in 1965, once sailed one from Fortaleza, in North Brazil, well over two thousand miles to Buenos Aires. But they demand great skill and experience, and disasters are not infrequent. The large *jangada* is used for fishing at some distance from the shore, up to the edge of the continental shelf, and is known therefore as the *jangada de alto*, or sometimes the *jangada de dormida* since on these longer voyages of several days the crew have to sleep on board in whatever comfort they can find.

Working sometimes on his own and sometimes as a crew member, the *jangada* fisherman of north-eastern Brazil reaps a difficult harvest. The skill and courage of the *jangada* crews as they navigate the treacherous waters is impressive, the more so since they are rewarded for their bravery by the smallest of catches.

The work calls for great skill, not only in handling the boat, but also in navigation. Even in the limited area of coastal waters fished from a single village, the catch may vary widely, from a small one to none at all. Among the arts of the fishermen – which every young man learns by example and experience, rather than by formal instruction – there is the important business of knowing the best fishing grounds. Fish may be plentiful in one place and completely absent in another. These are cherished and fiercely kept secrets, passed on within the group within the family.

Then there is the task of getting there. Fishermen find their way by an elaborate system of visual triangulation, based upon the observation and alignment of conspicuous landmarks. When the *jangada* passes out of sight of land, dead-reckoning is used instead, a rough, almost intuitive calculation of winds and currents, checked wherever possible by plumbline, and surprisingly accurate. All this calls for intelligence coupled with good eyesight and an excellent memory; the captain of a *jangada de alto* is a highly-qualified man and well deserves his greater share of the catch.

When a raft comes back, after a couple of days at sea under such difficult conditions, it seems a poor reward for such heroic exertions when, as frequently happens, there are only twenty or thirty pounds of fish to be shared out and sold. It is no rare thing for the catch to be less than the crew's subsistence needs during the voyage. The labors of the *jangadeiro* tend to be profitless. Although at times, high protein food crowds the ocean before him, he commonly suffers from malnutrition.

The problem is not simply a shortage of fish, which are seasonally plentiful. In the 1950's when an attempt was made to establish a more intensive fishing trade along the Brazilian coast, using Scandinavian boats and Brazilian crews, the experiment was technically successful: catches were much larger than had ever been achieved in the region. It was only abandoned because the enterpreneurs who would dispose of all this fish – chiefly through canneries – were afraid that by flooding the market the price of fish would drastically fall, their profits might suffer and their monopoly disappear.

The *jangadeiros'* problem is not so much the fish, as their means of getting them: the technique of fishing by handlines from *jangadas* is inefficient. *Jangada* fishing brings a small return but the fishermen are too poor, and too much at the mercy of the businessmen and the market, to adopt a more efficient technique. It is sometimes suggested that the *jangadeiros* continue to fish in their traditional and picturesque way, despite their hardships and poor returns, because they are natural conservatives, temperamentally contented with their simple way of life, quite indifferent to the modern world and its technological advances.

There may be some truth in this; but it is also sadly true that they are deprived of any real incentive to change by the economic system under which they work. Along with the hawkers or salesmen who buy and distribute the catch, they are obliged to register with the local authorities and pay a substantial tax to the fishermen's guild of which membership is compulsory. And the economy of a fishing village is not self-contained, but linked to the outside world in which they sell their fish

at fixed prices which have not kept pace with inflation. Although they can help along their basic trade by selling coconuts and by the products of their cottage industries – weaving straw baskets, for example, in some places – the overall balance of payments is never in the villagers' favor, and the *jangada* fishermen are seldom able to save any capital.

Other resources may be open to the *jangadeiro*: he may hold a little land, and gather a small harvest of coconuts, mangoes and cashews. But larger scale farming, even if it were possible, would be alien to him. A certain amount of subsistence fishing is possible in rivers, bays and lagoons, while mangrove swamps often yield crabs in abundance. A good haul of fish can also be taken with a beach-seine, a net some two thousand feet long, which is set parallel to the shore-line by a *jangada* and then hauled in from both ends. This net exactly resembles one used on the African coast, and is more productive than the use of hand-lines at sea; but since it is expensive, it is owned not by the fishermen themselves but by local farmers and planters, who take most of the profits.

The *jangada* fisherman is economically cornered, although he still gets some of the support he needs from a close-knit society, the extended family, the prosperity of the buoyant Brazilian economy passes him by. He is stuck there among the sand-dunes, in a village of mud huts roofed with palm-leaves, with little hope of improving his condition. Replacing the rafts themselves is a problem, for the *pau de jangada* logs have to be transported further and further to the coast from where they grow inland; the supply dwindles. They have to travel over longer distances and the cost goes up. The fishermen need capital, but their own savings cannot provide it, and the local enterpreneurs are seldom willing to risk investing in an activity so uncertain and poorly rewarded as *jangada* fishing. The outcome is inevitable. Increasingly, the *jangada*, cheaply built and locally owned, is being replaced by the expensive sailing-boat financed from outside the village, crewed by wage-earners instead of the owner's family and friends and justifying its higher cost by a far higher level of productivity. The fisherman loses his independence as well as his traditional craft and sees little of the real benefits of the change. He is forced to submit to it by economic pressures, by the rising cost of logs, the limited markets in his own area, and his inability to control prices.

And when he boards one of the many surviving *jangadas* and launches out once again for two long days of waterlogged exhaustion at sea, with the triangular sail flapping above him and the fish very slowly accumulating in his basket, he may possibly find comfort in the reflection that if there are any tourists around, and there are more of them every year, he is providing them with the material for some really splendid photographs. Or possibly, of course, not.

Guarani
Paraguay

In the great Paraguay-Parana basin, as well as along the southern coast of Brazil, live the Guarani, the southernmost branch of the once great Tupi-Guarani family of tribes. The Tupi-Guarani were dispersed throughout South America east of the Andes, from the mouth of the Amazon right down to the region of the River Plate. They are famous for their restless migrations, their warlike ways, and their practice of ritual cannibalism. The Guarani tribe itself is no exception.

Guarani history has from the 16th century been eventful. During the Spanish *conquista*, Guarani groups often joined the Europeans in their wars, at times even against Indians of their own language and culture. At other times, unbearably exploited, Guarani rebelled against European domination. Between 1609 and 1768 the Guarani were part of a 'Jesuit Republic' founded by missionaries in the region of the Parana and Uruguay rivers. Near the end of Jesuit rule there were nearly 150,000 Christianized Guarani. But after the expulsion of the Jesuits, decreed by the king of Spain, the missions

Many Guarani are practising Catholics after generations of intermarriage. They whisper confessions to priests through thin screens.

Guarani Paraguay

Only 2 per cent of Paraguay's population are pure Guarani. Away from the stiff military formality of Asunción, they farm and hunt in the forest.

This smuggler is constantly alert to planes, into which he can load his crates of contraband whisky appropriately called 'Smuggler'

This family of Guarani descent has an expensive transistor yet lives simply in a one-roomed shack on the edge of Asunción.

declined rapidly and soon most of the Guarani split up into small bands and turned back to primitive life in the forests. Yet they left their mark on Paraguayan culture. Widespread miscegenation between Guarani and the first Spanish settlers deeply marked the character of the Paraguayan people whose main language is still Guarani and whose culture bears many traits of Indian origin.

In the eastern forests of Paraguay there live today about 15,000 Guarani, remnants of this once populous tribe. A few thousand are left across the border in Argentina and in the Mato Grosso, and there are some groups in southern Brazil. They are split into three sub-tribes, each with its own dialect and distinguishing features: the Kayova, the Mbua, and the Nandeva. In addition there are the Guayaki, a small and very primitive tribe of eastern Paraguay who hunt and gather jungle fruits and berries. They are probably the remnants of the last phase before man took to agriculture.

Modern Guarani are scattered throughout an immense territory, some still in the heart of their aboriginal forest, others in close touch with peasants or even on the edge of cities. Nevertheless, all of them bear essential features of their spiritual culture, which makes for quite distinct characteristics.

There are no Guarani villages, for their houses, with gardens nearby, are isolated and scattered. They have perfectly adapted to their tropical forest homeland. They are experts on animal and plant life. They are mainly farmers, but nevertheless the men love hunting with bow and arrows and with a variety of traps and slings. The women like to roam through the forest gathering all kinds of edible plants and fruits. Their staple crop is maize, which among the Nandeva and the Kayova is also used for *chicha,* a fermented beverage popular at feasts. The Guarani also grow manioc, sweet potatoes, beans, cotton, tobacco and *urucu,* which gives a red dye for body painting, and also has medical and magical properties.

They live by what they grow. The phases of maize growing, from planting to harvesting, keep step with a cycle of magic rituals which culminate in a great feast when the first corn-cobs are brought in and blessed.

They hoard nothing except religious paraphernalia, weapons and tools for daily use, which are individually owned. A Guarani would never dream of amassing any kind of wealth; no-one would ever gain prestige based on material goods. This attitude is of course the Guarani's greatest handicap when he has to adapt to a modern economy.

The Guarani think that every life is punctuated by states of crisis which require rituals and specific precautions. After a birth, the father goes to rest in total isolation in his bed or hammock for about a week; he conforms to a rigorous diet and is forbidden to work. The Guarani believe that the father's behavior affects the infant's well-being. If he breaks the code, severe supernatural sanctions follow. Similarly, all girls at first menstruation remain isolated from family life for a month or so; their hair is cut and they are submitted to more or less the same restrictions as the father of a new-born child. Before puberty, groups of boys go through a complicated ritual with weeks of intensive religious exercises which culminate in the piercing of their lower lip; they too have a set diet. In the hole of the underlip they will always wear a small stick of resin or wood, a symbol of maturity and a magic defense against all evil.

Their sense of beauty is expressed less in ornamentation than in song and dance. Many of their rhythmic melodies recall their Jesuit past. Their myths and maxims are expressed poetically and are often rich in metaphors. Guarani patterns of tribal lore are the most beautiful of all the peoples of the jungle. They have no writing system and a simple technology, yet they have a bent for abstract thinking.

In principle, every Guarani may become a shaman, a combination of priest, magician, doctor and judge. He has to hear the call, to engage wholeheartedly in cult exercises and, whenever possible, to increase his knowledge of religious doctrine through frequent discussions with the great masters. Sooner or later inspiration will come: ritual chants invade the mind and give special power to exercise his profession. Dreams are full of these magic religious chants. They are gifts from heaven, and in time of trouble they are a great spiritual comfort. If you own a number of chants, you may assist at ceremonies and finally be recognized as a shaman and a religious leader of the community. There may be two or more shamans in one group, living in friendly and respectful competition; each one has his adherents, but they probably collaborate at the great tribal feasts. Guarani society is essentially egalitarian but nevertheless high religious status is a source of social prestige.

The shaman is often the only political leader of his community. Frequent religious exercises, fasting, sexual moderation and other observances strengthen his magical powers and intensify his communication with the divinities. He is a seer and receives messages from the gods. His wisdom makes him permanent adviser to his people; it is unthinkable that he should be disobeyed, unless he quarrels with a fellow shaman and is suspected of black magic. He wards off dangerous spirits and misfortunes and sickness, mainly with chants and tobacco. He blows a life-giving haze—the smoke of a sacred plant—onto the patient, while passing his hands over the patient's body to extract from it the substance or strange object that is causing the illness.

Above all he is a religious leader and conducts rituals and ceremonies. His chants are accompanied by dances. The men beat time with their gourd-rattles, while the women stamp thick bamboo rhythmically on the ground. Everyone sings and dances into a state of mystic rapture. Their souls go step by step through celestial regions, where they meet the different gods, each one in his domain. Every summer there is a time when the whole community dances, night after night, from sunset to sunrise, sometimes for months on end.

All three Guarani sub-tribes believe in a soul sent by the gods, which will join them in the afterworld to enjoy eternal happiness. The theory of the Nandeva sub-tribe is similar to that of all Guarani. They believe each man is born with two souls, a spiritual one sent from above at the moment of conception, and a second one of animal or earthly nature, whose germ was associated with the first one but which only reaches its full development through the sometimes bitter experiences of life on earth. The spiritual soul, called *aywu* or *nee*, which means 'speech', enables you to communicate with other humans; and it is the source of noble sentiments. The animal soul, *atsyygwa*, which means 'born out of pain', is responsible for man's temperament and for his biological reactions. You can predict someone's behavior if you know which animal species his *atsyygwa* belongs to. For example, a fussy frolicsome person may have a monkey *atsyygwa*, an angry one a jaguar *atsyygwa*, and the sluggard, that of a sloth. When you die the *aywu* returns to heaven, but the *atsyygwa* becomes an unhappy ghost, wandering nightly in the woods around the village. It is feared by the people, since you only have to catch a glimpse of it or hear its cry, and you will fall sick or even die.

For a Guarani human existence would be meaningless without daily mystic experience. As life on earth is but

Corned beef is one of Paraguay's main exports and the meat packing stations provide employment for many near Asunción.

a 'way of imperfections', all aspects of life are seen in the light of the supernatural, so there is nothing without a sacred character. In Guarani language there is no word for religion; when asked to translate it, the Indian might describe it simply as *nandereko*, 'our life, our way of being'. By frequent cult practice he hopes to reach a state of spiritual perfection which will enable the individual or even the whole community to be freed from the nasty realities of this doomed world, and to enter Paradise (without dying, if possible) in order to enjoy complete happiness through intense communion with the gods.

But religious doctrine is far from stable or uniform. Teaching varies from one sub-tribe to the other. Thus, the names of the gods and their attributes are different among the Nandeva, the Kayova and the Mbua, and important concepts in one sub-tribe may be absent in another. For instance, the Nandeva stick to a reincarnation theory which other sub-tribes are reluctant to believe. The Mbua could not believe that the Guarani's mythical hero brothers are twins, simply because for them the birth of twins is always a disgrace for the family and they would not be allowed to survive. Nevertheless Guarani religious doctrine contains a core of belief that makes for a unity of outlook in tribal religion.

The creation of the world, the divine twin heroes, the

Only a few of the Guarani now live their wandering traditional life, but even in the towns the old habits remain — like cigar smoking.

This prostitute is not behind bars but displays herself in her house which like many is fronted with wrought iron work.

Guarani lace work is called *nananti* — spider's web — and is famous throughout South America. It is made into mats, runners and wall hangings.

cataclysms of the past and the future, and Paradise: these are the chief myths of the Guarani, and mold their outlook on human existence. Some Guarani are deeply pre-occupied with the idea of the world's destruction in the near future. They interpret quite common events of nature as signs that the mythical prophecy is about to come true. The cataclysm may be another flood, a great fire, or both. Or perhaps the whole earth may be destroyed. Guided by its shaman, the whole community then migrates—towards sunrise—to some point on the Atlantic coast from which it will be easier to reach Paradise, the Land without Evil. There the group will live forever in perfect harmony and happiness, without illness or death. The image of Paradise depends on the shaman's visions. Some priests, influenced by the Jesuit teachings of the past, paint a picture like the biblical Eden.

The prophecy of a future cataclysm and Paradise probably came from original Guarani mythology, but it recalls St John's Apocalypse and other teachings of the Jesuit fathers. The blending of Indian and Christian stories brought about an overblown version which became obsessional. This is why messianic movements have been so frequent among the Guarani. Even today there are little bands of fanatical Guarani moving towards the Atlantic coast from which they hope to reach Paradise and so escape the menacing disaster.

111

Carnaval
Brazil

Salvador's *carnaval*, as elsewhere in Brazil, is more than a fiesta — it is a reassertion of an ancient right to life, joy and freedom.

The last days before Lent, the streets of Rio de Janeiro, like those in most other cities in Brazil, are given over to the people, who are dressed in butterfly costumes, and everyone has a song and a dance to perform. Barefoot boys beat out loud samba rhythms on old tin cans; and samba schools, whose thousands of dancers have practised for months in order to 'write their names on the asphalt' dance beneath the lights and eyes of a million onlookers. Sometimes the samba school processions are half a mile long. Out at the front are the officers of the school, dressed in silk hats and spats and carrying canes; and then come the dancers, each wing performing particular themes.

The school's standard-bearer twirls her flag of the samba school's colors – green and pink, or blue and white – followed by the *bateria*, the orchestra of hundreds of percussion players who pulse out a samba rhythm; and then, at last, the floats which depict the theme of the samba lyric. *Carnaval* is a huge extravagance when the people, like a gathering of bright tropical birds, celebrate their freedom in the space of two or three days and nights. They wear masks, spray one another with perfume, and become lost beneath the shouts and cries that fill the carnival street.

The richness and vitality of modern *carnaval* could hardly have been predicted from the early Portuguese-style *entrudo* which was little more than a few days free-for-all water-throwing in preparation for the dourness of Lent. Rio's 19th-century middle-class metropolis, with its carnival groups of students, bands and exclusive clubs parading classical allegories, was only gradually infused with the vitality of the favelas and the urban poor. From the very beginning it was black Brazil which provided the comedy and the color of *carnaval*. In Salvador and Recife in the north-east, the dramatically creative and popular carnival emerged from the slave regions of Brazil. A 19th-century visitor described groups of black slaves parading the streets of Rio in 18th-century courtiers' dress – precisely the style still worn today by the leading samba school dancers.

In north-east Brazil, unlike the southern USA, the negro slaves were commonly allowed to preserve their African cults and dances. This was not just out of benevolence, but rather as a means of distraction from the hardships of slavery – perhaps even as a means of controlling them. As the cities expanded and prospered, the African dances evolved and adapted to become yearly occasions and part of the carnival celebrations. In Recife carnival groups of dockers and carpenters and others came together like guilds. In Salvador a popular group in *carnaval* was the *afoxé*, made up of members of candomblé cults. Groups like these, playing traditional rhythms, are just as alive today. At *carnaval* they dressed dramatically in the costumes of the Indian and *caboclos* saints. Other less formal groups of equally long standing like *batuques* (the word first meant 'drummers') and 113

Carnaval Brazil

The preparations for *carnaval* have gone on for months before Lent. And then the explosion of exuberance will last only four days.

The street is filled with the thousands of samba school dancers who 'write their names on the asphalt' with Bacchanalian joy.

The mask is more than a costume; *carnaval* revellers in disguise cast off inhibitions and seize the moment to love — or even kill.

Group from the favelas flood the city dressed in their *fantasias*, spraying anyone they meet with a perfumed stimulant spray.

blocos ('blocks') improvised dances for their strolling players, who drank their way from house to house. They all used drums like the *stabaque,* and the high pitched bell-like *agogos,* and drew on Brazil's elaborate urban culture – a fusion of African, Indian and European – and notably on a dance called the samba. Full of subtly varied rhythms, it was around the samba that the world famous modern carnival was to develop.

Early in the 20th century, Rio became a Mecca for thousands of unemployed from the economically stagnant north-east. Whole city districts like Sáude and the Praça Onze were filled by immigrants from Bahia and Pernambuco. In these districts street corner *batuques* developed, reminiscent of those of Salvador, who played spontaneous sambas full of nostalgia for the north-east, reflecting the hardships of their new urban home. So important did the sambas, often held in candomblé cult houses, become that local dances were known as 'sambas.' The candomblé cult houses where popular sambas were held were to *carnaval* music what the riverboats in the southern United States were to traditional jazz.

The *semba,* as it was then pronounced, was brought to Brazil from Angola by slaves of Bantu origin and means 'belly button'. Its earliest form, still popular in Salvador's carnival today, was the *samba de roda* (samba in a wheel, or circle). The dancer of the moment would choose another from those singing and clapping around him or her. A belly-to-belly touch, once described as ideally producing a sound like a sugar crate snapping shut, was the signal for a change of dance. So vital is modern carnival, that new sambas are constantly being composed. Or the dancer may improvise or play with intricate steps while the music and rhythm is fixed. Like negro blues, which also originated in slave conditions, the songs, which are enormously varied and often untranslateable, tend to be saucy observations on life and love:

Solo: Woman with the great big basket . . .
Chorus: What a good basket!
Solo: Woman whose basket keeps on shaking . . . .
Chorus: Eh! What a basket!

In 1917 the first recorded samba took Rio's *carnaval* by storm, sweeping the traditional, more solemn polkas, waltzes and marches aside. This original samba was a comment on a police-chief's involvement with *jogo de bicho* (the animal game), an illegal form of gambling; but the recorded versions continuously omitted to mention the police and changed the game to roulette. Its authorship was hotly disputed by several samba composers and there were various versions of it. The creators of samba however rarely get a claim of their commercial profits.

By the 1930s Rio's favelas had expanded. Local samba groups, using percussion instruments and calling themselves samba schools, had begun to meet in the central Praça Onze where they would challenge each other to samba contests. Samba was already so popular that pressmen, politicians and tourist departments quickly appreciated their potential. Rules were laid down that every year samba schools should present a dramatized samba with a theme based on a part of Brazil's history, and in which the dancers would represent the leading characters. The tourist department appointed a panel of experts to judge the parade and select the winners.

Within a few years there were more than 40 samba schools, based mainly on individual favelas in Rio. Other less formal groups like the *blocos* faded into the background. Drink and record companies, politicians and even couturiers sponsored the carnival samba exhibitions so that they became increasingly lavish and frantically competitive. It was widely believed, with some justification, that the judges knew little about samba and were bribed. Samba themes became less cryptic, more bizarrely respectable and faithful to official Brazilian history – a history written almost exclusively by, about, and in the interests of, a privileged élite.

The conservative military regime which took power in 1964 was only too pleased to encourage all this. Samba had come a long way since it first expressed the ironies and sufferings of favela life. The people who subsidized *fantasias,* the carnival costumes, were the politicians, industrialists and slum landlords – the very people who profited from the favelas. Gradually Rio's glittering carnival has become a Roman style 'bread and circus'. It provides its participants with a brief, glorious fantasy; as it has been subsidized and exploited, it has lost a little of its authenticity. Back in Salvador and Recife the genius of popular carnival flourishes more freely. Here the traditional carnival clubs, *afoxés* and informal *blocos,* still release spontaneous *carnaval* and liberty on to the streets. Even the local samba schools, though modeled on those of Rio, are more authentic and creative, precisely because they are smaller, less formal and heavily inspired by the subtle rhythms of candomblé.

In Rio, the politicians are always eager to profit from people's need for release from the hardships of urban life. This is also true in Salvador and Recife, but here the pressures are still sufficiently weak, and traditions sufficiently strong, for the carnival to withstand the politicians' interest. Here *carnaval* is almost as vital and explosive as it has been in the past; the legendary *sambista* is a social reality. The man who quits an ill-paid job – or temporarily gives up hustling – to plunge himself and his meager savings, heart and soul into *carnaval,* with all its scope for music and dance, friendship and witty social comment knows that the legendary *sambista* is still alive. Women with children who somehow find time and money to make an eye-catching *fantasia* or a standard for the samba school believe in the carnival. They are artists, not just merry-makers. These are the people, however obscure and however changed the end-product in Rio, who keep true *carnaval* alive. 115

Villagers of Rio São Francisco
Brazil

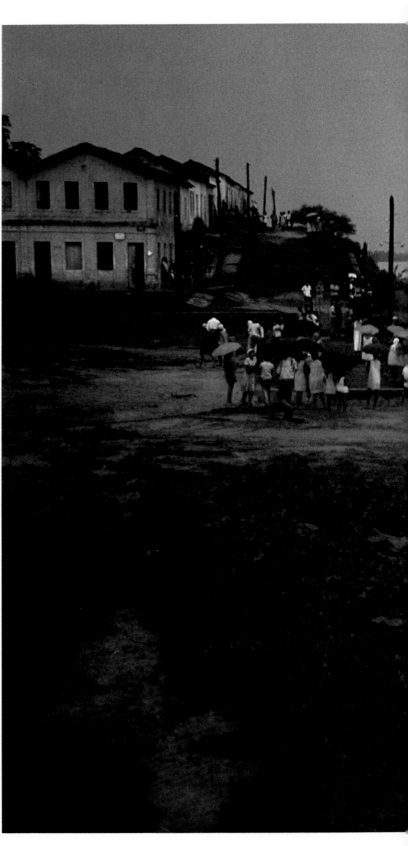

The great drought region of north-east Brazil is one of the most distressed regions of the world. It is called the *Sertão* and for generations its people have struggled to subsist with an almost constant scarcity of water. Their lands are arid semi-desert, largely covered in scrub forest and cactus and thorn bush. Droughts may last three years and, even in a 'good' year, the rain only comes in violent showers which turn the countryside a sudden green. Stream beds swiftly fill up, but they are soon dry. After a few days of the scorching sun, the earth has resumed its dusty brown. Little can grow; cattle are scrawny. The people of mixed Indian and Portuguese descent, are called *flagedlados*, the castigated ones.

It is through this vast, almost irredeemable region that the life-giving São Francisco river runs, over rapids, waterfalls and finally to the sea. On its margin, the annual

117

The Rio São Francisco links
1,800 miles of Brazil's
interior. Goods, news and
returning sons arrive by old
Mississippi paddle boats.

Rio São Francisco Brazil

The people of the parched *sertão* are called *flagedlados* – the castigated ones. A drought may last three years.

rise and fall produces a narrow flood plain where the soil conserves moisture. And here agriculture exists. But it cannot extend far inland. Irrigation is almost impossible because of the lie of the valley. The principal and most prosperous activity is cattle-grazing: along the riverbank, reaching far inland, there are great cattle *fazendas* (ranches). But the further inland they reach, the poorer and drier is the land. These are the contrasts of the region: for the *flagedlados* there can be little relief from a drought; for the people close to the river there is, at least, water.

The São Francisco river rises far in the south, in the mountains of Minas Gerais, and runs 1,800 miles in a long sweeping curve to Brazil's north-east coast. It is the longest river that flows entirely within Brazil's borders. Old wood-burning paddleboats, which could have steamed straight out of the pages of Mark Twain, still ply its lower reaches. But the river is navigable by these boats only between Pirapora and Juàzeiro, a distance of less than 800 miles. Along this course there are scores of towns and villages, each serving the paddleboats with wood, and many other stopping places besides, for fuel must be taken on four times a day. When the steamer stops, everyone comes out to watch; men, women and children. Even at stops which are apparently deserted except for a wood pile or an isolated farm, scores of

people will suddenly emerge from the scrub as if from nowhere. Beggars rush beneath the gangplanks to importune the tourists; women and children chatter on the riverside selling cakes and goat cheese. A 'half-hour' fuel stop can easily turn into two or three hours.

Sometimes it can be hard to distinguish the paddle-boats' crew from the passengers. Orders are rarely given; the decks are crowded with Brazilians keen to see their country, or young girls making friends with the crew, *flagedlados* escaping the droughts of the *Sertão* or even, on the down-river trip, men who have bought huge tracts of land in the north-east and who hope to make their fortune. The crew are assured of a good living on the boats and they make sure they know their job. Nobody, not even the captain, wears a uniform, but they are all proud of their boat. Four days out from Pirapora, the captain's skills are clear as he manoeuvres the boat through rapids, split-second turns in the rushing water, and round ugly rocks.

The river is an informal carriageway and so are the riverboats. But without them many of the towns and villages along the riverside could hardly survive at all. The boats carry many of life's essentials. They pick up the local produce—the great blocks of brown sugar, the corn and beans—which are then sold at Pirapora or Juàzeiro. Mail is delivered and passengers are carried. But the river is also the scene of other activity. There are government projects to open up the course to yet larger craft. There are plans to dredge and dam parts of the river to control its level, and other schemes with hydro-electric power stations set on the Alphonso Falls, a 260 foot wall of water below Juàzeiro, and on the headwaters above Pirapora. These are things that bring hope to the *flagedlados* and an impetus to the development of farming and grazing along the São Francisco.

The drought region of north-east Brazil, through which the river passes, is in sharp contrast to the humid tropical forest of the Amazon valley in the north. It is this region that gives the river much of its character. The herds of cattle which roam the thorny scrub are tended by *vaqueiros*—Brazilian cowboys—and on many of the *fazendas* they are permitted to own a portion of the increase of the herds under their care. But it is a rarely fulfilled generosity and the cowboys cannot be exclusively herdsmen. They clear small garden sites and plant maize, beans, manioc and cotton—only to find their meager agriculture destroyed by the lack of rainfall or the trampling of their cattle. The conditions of their lives are harsh and allow for little prosperity. Whatever the government relief schemes provide during periods of excessive drought, it is never enough. In 1958, some two million people in this region faced starvation as a result of the prolonged drought.

When things become so bad for *flagedlados* and *vaqueiros* that their cattle die and they are reduced to digging into the dusty stream beds for water the people,

Along the banks of the river
there are many centers of
pilgrimage, to which thousands
of devout Catholics come
from the surrounding *sertão*.

in their thousands, begin the long trek to the São
Francisco. The river is their ultimate savior. Somehow
they will scratch together the $3 for the trip upstream on
the riverboat; sleeping on deck on straw mats for seven
days; eating the leftovers of the first-class passengers
who had paid $25 for the same journey. From Pirapora
they carry on south to the plantations, or to Rio or
São Paulo where they look for work. Packed in trucks,
nick-named cockatoo perches, few of them have papers;
they are in the hands of labor contractors. The authorities seem to close their eyes to their fate. The city
favelas sometimes accommodate them; at other places
where they find work, they just sleep on the job when
their day is over. And then, if news comes through that
rain has fallen in the north-east, that the drought is over,
they begin the long journey home.

But in 1958 it was different. The *flagedlados* rebelled.
Instead of moving away to find work in the south, they
began to raid the nearest towns. They broke into houses
and shops in search of food. It was a minor revolution.
The apathy of other Brazilians was shattered. Suddenly
the entire country became aware of its north-eastern
region where 20 million people lived, and died, and
suffered terrible droughts. This was one of the reasons
for the attention paid to the São Francisco. Though, as

119

In a shrine city like Bom
Jesus da Lapa, life goes on
as normal, seemingly unaware
of the suffering caused by
drought in the *sertão*.

Rio São Francisco Brazil

When the rain comes, in sudden downpours, the dun *sertão* turns green in an hour. Roads become muddy, and the thin crops swiftly mature.

they say in these parts, 'every President builds a dam' to help with irrigation, progress is slow.

In other ways the river is a great benefactor. It has along its banks centers of religious pilgrimage to which thousands of pilgrims come each year. The shrine city of Bom Jesus da Lapa is perhaps the most famous, with its image of Christ, to which many miracles are attributed, and its church set in a cave. This shrine alone attracts more than 100,000 people every year. They come from all over the *Sertão*, from the mountains of Bahia and Minas Gerais, even from the furthest parts of the north-east, like Ceará and Rio Grande do Norte. They come by boat and steamer along the river, by truck and by foot from the arid interior, sometimes spending more than a month en route, and even by plane.

They are a strange people in this part of Brazil. The *flagedlados*, being of part Indian and part Portuguese descent, are stubbornly attached to their barren homeland. Between droughts, they say, it has a fine healthy climate and land is rich. Though they leave it with curses during the droughts, they always return. Their country is also a region that has inspired fanatic religious movements. Early in the 20th century Padre Cícero was excommunicated by the church, but was effectively the supreme spiritual and political leader of the *Sertão*. Even now many pilgrims flock to his tomb. But every movement is characterized by the appearance of a messianic leader pledged to lead his followers to a promised land. Perhaps the people could not live without such inspiration. They live in a hostile environment; they live under a semi-feudal yoke of *fazenda* cattle ranches; religious movements feed on the frustrations of these things.

The region has also produced numerous outlaw bands. One of the most famous was led by Virgílio Ferreira da Silva, and he and his *cangaceiros* were the terror of the whole region for 18 years until his death in 1938. The people would not believe he was dead until his severed head was displayed in several towns. Blind troubadours now sing folk verses in the market places of the *Sertão*, recounting his adventures and those of other *cangaceiros*. These outlaws were heroes of the poor, like Robin Hood. Just like religious fanaticism, banditry and its veneration seems a result of terrible frustrations in this harsh land.

The São Francisco river passes through these lands, and among these people. For those on the margin it is a ready supply of water, filtered through sand and gravel in huge earthenware pitchers. Children swim in the muddy waters; the piranha fish, which in the Amazon are reputed to be able to strip a cow in seconds, are harmless here. In the towns and villages along its way, the houses are poor; one room with only a few sticks of furniture and a picture of the Virgin. For the people of the arid interior, the São Francisco river is a way to the south. In times of desperation it is their artery, often the only means by which they can survive.

Along the course of the river there are scores of towns and villages. When the steamer stops, sleepy settlements burst into life.

For most of the people, home
is a one-room *adobe* hut with
a few sticks of furniture —
the Virgin's image
for the soul's comfort.

The paddle-boats must stop
for fuel four times a day.
Their appetites for wood are
voracious — but for stokers
it is a steady and envied job.

Favelas of Rio de Janeiro
Brazil

Throughout the whole of South America, the plains, the forests and mountains have been emptying their people into the cities at a rate unparalleled by any other continent in history. It began in the 1940s. A decade later the socio-economic crisis was engulfing virtually all the countries of South America. In Peru, hundreds of thousands of Indians, many of them not speaking Spanish, have stampeded into the packed cities. In Argentina, which is a third the size of the US and twenty times bigger than Britain, over seven million of its twenty-four million people inhabit the single conurbation of Buenos Aires.

They arrive illiterate amid the jungle of factories and skyscrapers, slums, television, trade unions, football, politics. For many years, some two million have been joining the potential work force of the cities every year. Most of them live in shanty towns and tenements and slums clinging to the hillsides.

Some are overwhelmed. The thick peasant's body stretched across the mosaic pavement beneath the skyscrapers at the corner of Rio Visconde de Inhuama and Rio Branco street that I came across on my last visit to Buenos Aires was like the jetsam of a tidal flood. It lay, where he had rested and died, all day in the din of traffic and rushing feet. The fastest growing city in the world this century has been Brazil's Sao Paulo. In 1874 its population was 25,000, in 1920 579,000, in 1947 it was 1,776,000, in 1960 it was 3,825,251. A decade later it was over 6.5 million. Buenos Aires, the largest city in Latin America, has a population of over 7 million. A century ago it was under 100,000. The pattern of bewildering expansion, above all since the 1940s, has been the same throughout the half-continent.

Such an influx has combined with an onrush of literacy to produce an explosion of want. Unlike their Asian counterparts, all are swept into the acquisitive hedonism of western civilization. In Venezuela, literacy leapt from fifty to eighty per cent during the first half of the 1960s. A comparable increase was recorded in Brazil. In an advanced urban setting, the written word comes like light to the blind; and amid a people who traditionally daubed their politics on every smooth vertical surface, the very walls bludgeon them with ideas.

There is no city in South America without its shanty areas, its slums, its favelas (as the Brazilians call them). In Venezuela, they are *los barrios*. Caracas, Venezuela, is a city of skyscrapers and nice villas under siege by its own slums. The rich, respectable city lies along a rift valley between two parallel ranges, the last cadence of the Andes. The slums, *los barrios,* cluster thickly on the precipitous hillsides like tented barbarians. Day by day, from the city below, the black window holes make them look lifeless and abandoned. At nightfall their lights prickle the darkness on both flanks of the city – *la cintura hambriente* (the hungry belt). Government after government has attempted to clear them, or to rebuild

Overlooked by the vast statue of Christ at Corcovado, many of Rio's people live in unalleviated poverty in their makeshift hillside favela.

Only one in four of favela
children go to school. Flavio
does not. Yet the growth of
basic literacy has been fast,
and ideas are spreading.

A large room in a favela
shack is 6ft by 10ft; the
parents and five children
share one bed. Another two
children sleep in a cot.

in gridded concrete where the shacks of boarding, metal
drum and mud inhabited by some 400,000 Caraquenhos
have stood for decades.

In a two-room shack propped on stilts against the
eroding hillside, an old woman lives with her daughter
and five grandchildren on a small handful of money a
week, less than a twentieth of what the oil companies
pay one average, overalled Venezuelan employee. The
shack has been her home for twelve years. She sits on a
box on the earth floor. Water comes once a week by lorry,
two and a half dollars a barrel, to be carried up from the
road in biscuit tins by the children. There is electricity,
and an electric iron, and a wireless. Some neighbors
have television; but these tiny intrusions of easy life
do little more than sharpen the difficult realities. Of her
own eleven children, the old woman knows the where-
abouts of only three. Only one of the grandchildren, the
clever one, attends school regularly.

At the foot of the hillside a group of children plays in
the trench where the *barrios'* open drains empty. One is
a cripple who rolls around on his rump like a weighted
doll that cannot topple over. Along the wall opposite,
adjoining the fine church, a pro-government slogan had
been daubed – perhaps by the police – 'Hunger and
misery are the heritage of Communism – death to
Fidel (Castro)'.

Probably the worse slums are Brazil's favelas. They

Death is seldom far; mourning is a common function of the living. Dysentery is the big killer; but malnutrition is on the side of every infection.

Before he was born, Mano's parents migrated to Rio de Janeiro from their village in the *sertão*, exchanging one poverty for another.

are certainly the most famous – almost romantically depicted in the film *Black Orpheus,* and the diary of a mother who lived in a São Paulo favela published as *Beyond All Pity.* But the story is the same among the *barriadas* of Peru, and the *callampas* of Chile. At the northern end of Salvador, the old capital of Brazil's north-east, it is the mud flats of the northern end, the *alagados,* that have become the slums. Here, a hundred thousand people live in flimsy houses of stolen boarding, precariously linked by narrow cat-walks over eddying water that is murky with sewage and factory chemicals. Every year the district grows, feeling its way further along the mud flats. Vultures circle above it, living on its garbage.

It is Rio's favelas, however, that – like Caracas's *barrios* – look down from high above on the glittering city. The poorest shacks of all are on the steepest ground; their foundations are least certain, and in high rain or fierce wind they can slide. Houses rarely consist of more than one room, and they are built of wooden crates, cardboard and corrugated iron. The people have no legal title to the land on which their homes are built. The inhabitants are perpetually at the mercy of diseases propagated by overcrowding and bad or absent sanitation; by the hunger that comes from too few jobs, too little pay, and by the mere presence of too many people. Only one in four favela children goes to school. The larger the favela the greater its problems. It was estimated that in the early 1960s some ten thousand favela children in Rio alone died of dysentery.

Favela people see themselves as much a part of the city as anyone else. Their ambitions and even their occupations are the same as the city dwellers'. It is their poverty that sets them apart. Yet the favelas are themselves as much a part of city life as any other precinct. They are in their way as integrated into the city as the skyscraper blocks and factories. In Rio they can be found, constantly changing and shifting in every zone – from the drab industrial north among all the factories, to the swanky, commercial middle-class south. They sprout on level ground as well as on hills. Sometimes their spread and clutter is appalling, sometimes they are well laid out. Their development, decline and redevelopment are closely linked with the economic fortunes of the city itself.

The favela people are by no means all migrants who have flooded into the cities with their innumerable children from the interior. Nor indeed are they the only urban poor. In most Latin American cities there are just as many living in comparable hardship in other types of housing, in rack-rented tenements, cramped back alleys and wooden houses. The move to a favela can sometimes be a step up in the world. And one must discount the popular notion that they live half-apathetically, half-romantically within their culture of poverty. Their very roots are insecure. They are constantly liable to be

moved on. They stay at the discretion of the actual owner of the land – perhaps a national of the country itself, or a large corporation, or possibly even a municipality. There is little incentive to build permanent dwellings. If the land is not too steep, it could easily be

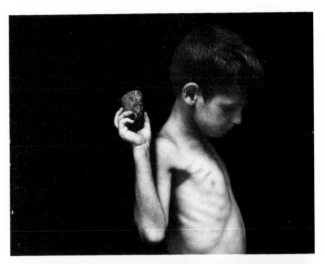

Favela dwellers have no legal title to their shacks, even though they change hands for cash. José (and his son Zacarias) could be moved out.

Favelas Brazil

Few favelas have any drainage or piped water. Normally drinking water must be bought from a tanker and carried home in tin cans.

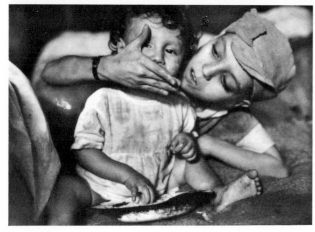

taken over for new residential houses for a different class, or a new hotel. Those moved on simply shift to another of the city's favelas.

New favelas are forever springing up. Small favelas tend to grow. In Rio de Janeiro, the largest of all, Jacarèzinho, had a population of more than a hundred thousand in the early 1970s. It has been proved long ago that razing favelas to the ground cannot remove the underlying reasons for their existence. Somewhere between fifteen and thirty per cent of Rio's people are in no position to find anything better for a home than a shack in a favela.

The larger favelas are often like a town within a town. Some actually have their own businesses, shops and services, creating an internal labor market. Most work in the factories beneath, along the perimeter of the favela – some forty per cent of the work force of Rio's Jacarèzinho are so employed; and the growth of Barreira do Vasco, also in Rio's north zone, is largely the result of labor demands of the neighboring Coca-Cola and Mercedes-Benz plants.

It is in the favelas and their like that the political prophets perceive – probably mistakenly – the seeds of revolution.

28

A 12-year-old boy feeds his 17-month-brother. Both their parents are out at work. In South America, slum birthrates are over 3%.

For Mario and Flavio from the
favela, the dreamland of
Rio's shops is only a few
hundred yards away — but,
like the sea — seldom visited.

129

Glossary to the peoples of lowland South America

The population of the South American continent has one of the highest rates of growth in the world. In 1960 there was an estimated 140 million: by 1969 this figure had already swollen to an estimated 186 million.

Medicine is perhaps the chief reason for this growth. The World Health Organization and other agencies have promoted mosquito control, which has eliminated malaria from large areas of the continent. Yellow fever is no longer a main cause of death in the tropical regions. Gastro-intestinal diseases due to poor hygiene – the principal cause of death in most South American countries – are being reduced as literacy rates increase and more people become aware of basic health rules. So the death rate has slowed down. Meanwhile rigorous application of Catholic dogma has helped keep the birth rate as high as ever. Another basic reason for the population explosion is immigration.

The history of immigration to South America goes back several hundred years to 1494 when Spain and Portugal divided the continent. Spain took the west, Portugal the east, and then both largely ignored their vast new lands until the 16th century when the French, the English on the lower reaches of the Amazon, and the Dutch all along the northern coastlines, began to take an interest in the neglected continent. The Portuguese staked a firm claim in the face of this competition to a huge chunk of the continent east of the Andes. Immigrants began to arrive from Portugal, and settled mostly on the northern part of what is now Brazil. When the local Indians proved unsatisfactory laborers for the newcomers, large-scale transportation of slaves from Africa was begun – probably over four million of them. But more recently voluntary immigration has helped swell the continent's population.

Despite the increasing number of new arrivals in South America, vast tracts of the interior have stayed untouched. On average, the continent is still sparsely peopled, with only 20 people to each square mile. Much of the hinterland of Brazil is looked upon as uninhabitable. The plains of Argentina are suitable for only a handful of adventurous ranchers and their sheep.

Most of the population is concentrated along the coastline and along the river banks, though the new roads that are being carved inland through the forests attract settlement in the same way as the wide rivers did in the days of the early pioneers. 80% of the continent's inhabitants live within 300 miles of the sea.

The seaboard cities of Buenos Aires, Montevideo, Rio de Janeiro, São Paulo and Caracas are densely populated and attract the highest proportion of immigrants. Buenos Aires, including its suburbs, has the highest population of any city in the southern hemisphere. São Paulo claims to be the world's fastest growing city. Over half Venezuela's total population concentrates around Caracas. Towns continue to expand with frantic

energy: new wealth is one result; squalid shanty towns (or favelas), huddling on the edges of the big cities, are another. But despite the drift to the cities in the 1940s and 1950s (largely due to the deliberate promotion of industrialization) the total populace remains predominantly rural.

Miscegenation has been widely practised, by the diverse peoples who came to South America, for over four hundred years. Over half the population is of mixed descent, stemming from the three primary races of Amerindian, negro and European. Nevertheless, there remains great ethnic diversity, and it is easy to divide areas into roughly distinct cultural and racial brackets.

Even Brazil, for all its much publicized ethnic mingling, and with a 92.3 million population that perhaps comes nearest to the idea of a 'cosmic race', is ethnically divisible. In the north, people of Amerindian, African, and Portuguese stock predominate, while it is to the south that recent European arrivals – from Scandinavia, Germany, Italy – tend to go. The Japanese came at first chiefly to the commercial centres, but their spirit of enterprise has led many of them to brand-new markets, some of them agricultural, inland.

The pampas countries of Argentina (over 25 million inhabitants) and Uruguay (under 3 million) contrast with the rest of 'Spanish' South America, since they have a European element of over 90%, largely of Spanish and Italian origin. In both countries less than 3% are Indians, and the negro percentage is negligible.

Paraguay (2.4 million inhabitants) differs again in being overwhelmingly (97%) *mestizo* most of them descendants of Guarani Indians and 16th century Spanish settlers. They present tiny percentage of Japanese people is expected to increase under an agreement made in 1959 to allow the immigration of 85,000 during the succeeding 30 years, with an annual quota of 3,500.

The three Guianas differ in ethnic content since they have a substantial East Indian element, which originated mostly from Madras and Calcutta and now amounts to over 43% in Guyana and 24% in Surinam. The mulatto and negro element in both these countries is over 40%. Europeans, Chinese and Amerindians make up the remainder.

The Indian (i.e. American Indian) population is broadly described on pages 12 and 13. In the tropical Amazonian forest basin, from central Venezuela to the mouth of the Amazon, live farm villagers of the Arawak, Tupi, Carib and Jivaro families. Some are settled, others semi-nomadic. Their agriculture is slash-and-burn: they clear some forest, burn the stumps, sow the crop, and move on when the soil is eroded. Men usually hunt and fish, while women tend the crops. Their houses are large, usually thatched, and either round or rectangular. Cannibalism was common, and the Tupi tribes especially were famous warriors. Warfare was continuous. Some tribes practised and still practise scalping, head hunting

COUNTRY	POPULATION	
ARGENTINA	25,040,000	
BOLIVIA	5,062,000	
BRAZIL	92,240,000	
CHILE	10,151,000	
COLOMBIA	21,265,000	
ECUADOR	6,510,000	
FRENCH GUIANA	49,000	
GUYANA	740,000	
PARAGUAY	2,395,000	
PERU	13,586,000	
URAGUAY	2,945,000	
SURINAM	4,000,000	
VENEZUELA	11 000 000	

Legend:
- Amerindian
- Mestizo - - - - mixed blood, Amerindian and European
- European Stock
- Mulatto - - - - mixed blood Negro and European
- Negro
- Zambo/Cafuso - - - - mixed blood Amerindian and Negro (known as Zambo in Spanish speaking countries, and Cafuso in Brazil.)
- **GUYANA** The 52% Asian community derived from China Java and India
- **SURINAM** The 47% Asian community derived from China and the East Indies

Many nations contributed to South America's population in the past 500 years with the result that it is now one of the most varied in the world.

and head-shrinking. Villages are often on river-banks. Clothing is scant, but they wear ornaments of feathers, bone and shell. They often paint and tattoo their bodies, and deform their ears and lips.

The other common type of Indian east of the Andes is the nomadic hunter and gatherer who hunts in bands across the pampas of Patagonia and northern Argentina, or roams up and down the great rivers. (Forest hunters like the Mura and Nambicuara are similar in culture to the pampas hunters). They have no permanent villages, but they have well-defined areas. Technology is simple. They usually make fire by drilling. Most wear skins, and live in conical huts like the North American tepee, or under lean-to wind-shelters.

The Indian population originated from Asia. They migrated down through the bottle-neck of Central America. Some, after settling in South America, went north again – to the Caribbean islands. But large-scale migration has now ceased. Disease and extermination is ever decreasing their numbers. Many follow the white man to the cities, where they merge, or rather submerge, in the non-Indian population.

NON-INDIAN MINORITIES

BUSH NEGROES OF SURINAM AND CAYENNE *Population:* over 50,000. Language groups: various. From 1538, negro slaves were brought to South America to work on the plantations. Most Bush Negroes, who include the Boni, Djuka and the Paramaka, live along the coast of Surinam (formerly Dutch Guiana) and up the river Maroni, where they have limited relations with the Indian tribes. Their strong culture maintains West African elements. Their staple diet is cassava and fish. They live in carved and painted houses, sometimes on stilts, and build graceful canoes. They tattoo their stomachs and worship ancestors and spirits.

EAST INDIANS Some 46% of Guyana's 834,000 population are of East Indian origin – descendants of indentured laborers brought between 1837 and 1917 to work on sugar plantations. A comparable proportion (40%) of Surinam's 431,000 population is similarly derived.

LEVANTINES A significant minority of people of Arab – mostly Levantine – origin, as well as Armenians, are well established in urban Brazil and elsewhere.

ENGLISH OF ARGENTINA English immigrants came to the Argentine at the end of the 19th century. They settled in districts around Buenos Aires, such as Hurlingham, and imposed a still recognizable pattern of English customs, schools and clubs on upper-class Argentine society. There is a significant English and Scottish ethnic presence also in Brazil.

GERMANS Throughout South America, people of German ancestry – for example, Paraguay's long-standing leader Alfredo Stroessner – have excelled in many fields, especially business and politics. Between 1850 and 1950, Germans accounted for 3% of Brazil's immigration.

ITALIANS In Uruguay and Argentina, which contrast with the rest of South America in that about 90% of their populations are of European descent, the people are of mainly Italian – particularly Neapolitan – and, of course, Spanish stock. In Brazil, Italians accounted for 33% of the vast immigration that took place between 1850 and 1950.

JAPANESE OF BRAZIL *Population:* 630,000 of which 170,000 were born in Japan, and 460,000 are second generation. Japanese farmers' sons were attracted to Brazil as coffee workers at the end of the 19th century. They proved so highly skilled and successful that they changed the whole pattern of Brazilian agriculture, introducing rice, pepper and jute. Their children are now moving into commerce and politics. Most are still concentrated in São Paulo state.

JAVANESE OF SURINAM *Population:* 43,000. Language group: Javanese. In 1891 Javanese workers were brought to work on the plantations of Surinam (formerly Dutch Guiana). They now represent 16% of the country's population and have remained generally separate from the other races. They live in extended family groups, and work their land for a subsistence. Wet rice is their chief crop, but many live and work in towns. Their marriages are frequently arranged by parents. They are mostly Muslim and circumcise their male children between the ages of 10 and 16.

NEGROES *Population:* unknown. Language groups: various. To compensate for the falling supply of Indian labor, negro slaves were introduced into Brazil, Colombia and Venezuela towards the middle of the 16th century for the hard work of sugar production. In Brazil they were especially useful for their technological knowledge – of iron smelting, for example. Generally there were restrictions against intermarriage between Europeans and negroes, except in Venezuela where a creole population emerged. In Colombia negroes now outnumber whites in lowland areas. Throughout South America, they hold all types of job.

INDIANS

ACHAGUA *Population:* unknown. Language group: Arawak. Members of the Achagua tribe, which is divided into clans, live in the grassland areas of Colombia in fenced-off villages of round communal houses and a men's clubhouse. Men clear fields and hunt with arrows tipped with curare poison. Women grow sweet potatoes, maize, beans and manioc, and make pottery. Men are allowed several wives, brought in from other villages. The Achagua have in in the past been attacked by the Guahivo (q.v.).

AGUANO *Population:* unknown. Language group: probably Panoan. The Aguano live in the Loreto district in the Montana region of Peru in villages made up of communal houses occupied either by families of daughters and their elderly parents, or by sons living with their wives' families. They are mostly riverside villages and the people catch fish and grow manioc and maize.

AHAPOVO (see ARIKEM)

AMAHUACA *Population:* 100–250. Language group: Panoan. The Amahuaca group of tribes live between the Ucayali river in Peru and the Jura river in Brazil, in one-house villages in which the people – who are mostly related – live communally. They make pottery, and grow maize and manioc, but hunting is their most important source of food. Mothers often strangle babies at birth, a practice which is the main threat to the tribes' survival.
(pages 32-37)

AMANAYE *Population:* about 50. Language group: Tupi-Guarani. The tribes of the Amanaye live in houses with thatched, gabled roofs, in villages near the Tocantis river in the Para district of Brazil. They use dugout canoes on the rivers and catch turtles and fish. They grow cotton to weave, and the men hunt. Only chiefs have more than one wife.

APALAI *Population:* 100–250. Language group: Carib. The Apalai tribes live in settled villages in the Brazilian state of Amapa, north of the Amazon estuary. Men take their wives from outside their own villages and their immediate locality. For food, the tribes depend on their agriculture rather than on hunting and fishing.

APIACA *Population:* over 500. Language group: Tupi-Guarani. This tribe who live in the state of Mato Grosso in Brazil, has integrated with others nearby and may soon be extinct. The remaining Apiaca grow manioc, maize, peanuts, pumpkins and cotton. Women do most of the hard agricultural work and the men hunt and fish from bark canoes. Only headmen may have more than one wife. The village consists of only one very long, thatched house made of bark or palm and large enough for several hundred people. Each village is independent, but people can move freely from one to another.

APINAYTE *Population:* 100–250. Language group: Ge. Most of the Apinayte live in the Para district of Brazil, are now settled, and have become integrated into nearby tribes. They grow manioc as their staple crop, and sweet potatoes, gourds and cotton; and they hunt animals. They make dugout canoes and share agricultural work: men clear the land; women help to plant and harvest. Their villages consist of several large houses arranged in a circle and occupied by families related to each other through the female line. Villages are divided on a clan basis, into two sections.

ARARA *Population:* unknown. Language group: probably Carib. Little is known about the Arara tribes except that they are still hostile nomads who live in the Para state of Brazil. They do not rely on agriculture, but hunt and gather for their staple foods. Although there are several rivers nearby, they apparently have no canoes.

ARAWAK (or LOKONO) *Population:* unknown. Language group: Arawak. The Arawak live along the coastal strip of Guyana and Surinam cultivating, fishing and hunting for their food. They are known for their fine basketwork, pottery and weaving. They used to keep slaves. On marriage, a man goes to live with his wife's parents and works for them.

ARIKEM (or AHOPOVO) *Population:* unknown. Language group: Tupi-Guarani. Living on the borders of the Mato Grosso, Rondonia and Amazonas states of Brazil, this small tribe cultivate manioc and maize. Their villages are made up of two communal houses together with a special hut in which they keep the bones of ancestors.

ARUA (see MACURAP)

ASHLUSLAY *Population:* unknown. Language group: Matacoan. The Ashluslay live on the west Paraguayan Chaco. Sometimes called Chalupi, they grow maize and manioc. Both men and women do the agricultural work: Their horses, sheep and cattle were introduced originally by the Spanish. Villages are made up of houses, inhabited by several families, facing the village street or plaza. They weave on looms and make pottery.

ASURINI (see YURUNA)

AUETO *Population:* 250–300. Language group: Tupi-Guarani. Most of this group of tribes living in the Mato Grosso state of Brazil has now become extinct. The Kamayura, who are the largest surviving tribe, live in houses with high thatched roofs in which several families live together. Villages are led by a headman and remain independent of the tribe's other settlements. They grow tobacco and eat as staple foods, manioc, maize, peanuts, beans, and peppers supplemented with fish, meat and gathered foods. The Aueto are known for their extensive trade with other tribes. Kamayura shamans impersonate spirits and re-enact tribal myths.

AWEIKOMA (see CAINGANG)

AWETI One of the two tribes of Tupi origin that now live in the Xingu National Park (q.v.).

BACAIRI *Population:* 250. Language group: Carib. This tribe, of the Mato Grosso **13**

state of Brazil, has had much contact with Europeans. They use slash-and-burn farming techniques to grow sweet manioc, maize and sweet potatoes. The men are responsible for clearing and burning the land, while women plant and tend the crops. Men marry very young girls, and the people live in houses large enough for several families, arranged around a village plaza with a special guest hall in the middle. The Bacairi trade with other tribes in tobacco, cotton and baskets. Each village has a headman who may be succeeded by a son.

BANIWA *Population:* 1,000–1,500. Language group: Arawak. A large number of tribes make up the Baniwa, who live on the borders of north Amazonas in Brazil and Colombia. They fish and hunt for food and grow manioc, the men clearing the ground and the women then tending the crops. Villages consist of one large communal house. Many Baniwa are noted for their skill as potters.

BARASANA (see TUCANO)

BORORO *Population:* 500–1,000. Language group: Bororo or Ge. Once one of the major tribes of central Brazil, these people now live in the Mato Grosso state of Brazil. The Bororo hunt, fish and gather seeds and berries, and, despite contact with Europeans, they do not practise agriculture. They live in conical huts in the dry season and build ridge-roofed dwellings sometimes on piles for the wet season. Their houses are always built in a circle

around the men's house. Villages are led by headmen, with chiefs above them. Rank and wealth are inherited not from the father, but from the mother's brother.

BOROWA (see MACU)

CAINGANG *Population:* 3,000–4,000. Language group: Ge. The Caingang, who include the Aweikoma, form one of the largest groups in south Brazil and north Paraguay. They have had contact with Europeans for over a century. Groups are widely scattered; they make little use of rivers and live off the land. In bands they hunt peccaries, tapirs and jaguars. They now build houses with gable roofs. The villages are ruled by headmen; shamans guide village policy. Although there are various chiefs, who gain prestige by distributing gifts to the headmen, they hold little real power.

CAMARACOTO *Population:* over 500. Language group: Carib. Most of the tribes live in Venezuela in the southern Amazonas and, Bolivar, while some live in Brazil. They live in villages of thatched, irregular houses., and grow crops on land cleared and planted by the men.

CANELO (or NAPO) *Population:* unknown. Language group: probably Zaporoan. The Canelo live on the borders of Napo Pastaza and Santiago Zamora in Ecuador. Little is known about them. They have integrated with other tribes and have lost many of their old customs.

CANICHANA *Population:* unknown. Language group: Canichana. Living in palisaded villages between the junctions of the Rio Guapore and the Rio Mamore in Bolivia, the Canichana tribe base their diet on fish and game, and practise only a little agriculture.

CAQUETIO *Population:* unknown. Language group: Arawak. The Caquetio live on the north coast of Venezuela, east of

Lake Maracaibo. They grow maize, manioc, and sweet potatoes, supplementing their diet by hunting and fishing. They trade extensively with other tribes and obtain gold from the Jirajara. Their houses are thatched and are situated near the fields. Their society is class-structured, with nobles, wealthy people and commoners. Men may have more than one wife. Paramount chiefs, thought divine, rule over small states and are succeeded by their sons.

CARAIBA: The name which many Indian people call the white man.

CARAJA *Population:* 2,000. Language group: Caraja. The Caraja live along the Rio Araguaia in the Brazilian states of Goias and Para and on the borders of Mato Grosso and are traditional enemies of the Shavante (q.v.). They use dugout canoes to catch fish and turtles. The men grow manioc by the slash-and-burn method. Villages, built on the river banks, consist of several rectangular houses with arched roofs. Each has a men's house separated from the main main part of the village by a plaza. When married (preferably with one of his maternal cousins) a man lives with his wife's family. Headmanship of a village passes from father to son. Villages combine to hold large ceremonies.

CARIB *Population:* over 5,000. Language group: Carib and others. Most surviving members of the many Carib tribes are found in Brazil and Guyana. Different tribes place different emphases on agriculture, fishing and hunting, but nearly all grow manioc and catch fish. Men clear the land and make baskets; women harvest crops and make pottery. They use either dugout or bark canoes. Tribes near the coast build their houses on piles. All Caribs thatch their houses. The men prefer marriage with a paternal cousin, and many marry several sisters. Until his first child is born, a man lives with and works for his bride's father. Villages are ruled by headmen with limited power, and are autonomous.

CARIJONA *Population:* unknown. Language group: Carib. Probably few in number, the Carijona live in the Caquet and Amazonas regions of Colombia. They grow manioc as their staple, and hunt and fish. Women till the soil and make pottery. All live together in one large village house. The tribe is divided into clans based on descent from male ancestors. They marry outside both clan and village.

CASHINAWA *Population:* 250–500. Language group: Panoan. The Cashinawa, who live in the basin of the Jurna and Purus rivers of Amazonas state in Brazil, possess no domestic animals, but hunt and fish and practise intensive agriculture. On land prepared by the slash-and-burn method they grow crops like maize, manioc, beans, peppers, tobacco and cotton. Once the men have cleared the land and planted the crops, the women are responsible for the rest of the work. They prefer marriage with a first cousin. Headmen may have more than one wife. A newly-married man goes to live in his wife's house. All houses are thatched, and large enough for many families.

CATUKINA *Population:* 1,000–2,000. Language group: Catukinan and Panoan. In the Acre and Amazonas regions in Brazil, near the Jaruna river and its tributaries, the many Catukinan tribes live by agriculture, hunting and fishing. They grow maize, sweet manioc and peanuts. Villages consist of a single, large, thatched, beehive-shaped house. The houses of the Mangeroma, most famous of these tribes, are vast and cone-roofed, often 150 feet round, 40 feet high, and are said to hold up to 250 people.

CAWAHIB *Population:* over 300. Language group: Tupi-Guarani. Spread over a large area of the Brazilian states of Rondonia and Amazonas, many of the tribes are now extinct. Those who survive neither keep domestic animals nor practise crafts, but grow cotton, peppers, maize, beans and manioc, and hunt and fish and gather nuts are berries. They travel in bark canoes. They prefer marriage with a first cousin. Only headmen are allowed more than one wife, usually sisters. Headmen are succeeded by a son, and villages are inhabited chiefly by families related to each other through the male line. Sometimes chiefs emerge through the conquest of other villages.

CAYAMO (see Northern CAYAPO)

Northern CAYAPO (or CORA)
Population: 2,000–3,000. Language group: Ge. The Northern Cayapo are widely dispersed in the Brazilian states of Para and Mato Grosso. They include the Cayamo, Mentuktire, Xikrin and Diore. Staple foods are bitter and sweet manioc, sweet potatoes and maize. They also hunt, fish and gather fruits and berries. Apart from basketwork, the Cayopo have no crafts although they grow cotton. Villages are divided into two portions, one for each of the two matrilineal clans. Their houses are long and communal, and are centred around a bachelors' house. They have strict rules forbidding plural marriages. Marriages are arranged with a bride from the opposite clan by parents long before the children reach puberty. After marriage men go to live with their bride's parents. Villages are ruled by two headmen and a council. Both sexes are graded by age. A Cayapo man does not gain full adult status until he has killed a man.
(pages 22–31)

Southern CAYAPO *Population:* unknown. Language group: Ge. The Southern Cayapo live in Minas Gerais and Goias in Brazil, and have their own distinctive language. In contrast to the Northern Cayapo (or Coroa) the men are allowed several wives. They grow maize as their staple crop.

CHALUPI (see ASHLUSLAY)

CHAMA *Population:* unknown. Language group: Panoan. Living along the Ucayali river in eastern Peru, the tribes of the Chama cultivate sweet manioc, maize, peppers, cotton and tobacco. They also hunt, fish and catch turtles. Women make pottery, weave and till the land cleared by the men. Men live and work for their bride's family after marriage. They are allowed several wives: either sisters, slaves or women captured in war. Several families, related through females, live in villages consisting of one communal house. Each settlement is independent with no higher political authority or link.

CHANDRI (see CHANDULE)

CHANDULE (or CHANDRI) *Population:* unknown. Language group: Tupi-Guarani. The members of this tribe live in villages of thatched houses scattered among the islands of the La Plata Estuary in Uruguay, fishing and cultivating maize as their staple food.

CHAPACURA *Population:* 800–1,000. Language group: Chapacuran. Most of the Chapacura tribes are extinct, but those that survive are scattered through the Brazilian states of Rondonia and Amazonas. They hunt, collect turtle-eggs, fish, and grow sweet manioc (their main food) peppers, pineapples and maize. They use either bark or dugout canoes, and make bark cloth, pottery and weave. Their houses, which hold several families, are built as lean-to's, partially covered with palm-leaf mats.

CHIQUITO *Population:* unknown. Language group: Chiquitoan. Many of the Chiquito tribes remain uncontacted by Europeans at the time of writing, and live in Santa Cruz in Bolivia. Many have been heard of only by name from other Indians. Those who are known live mainly by growing maize, sweet manioc and potatoes and by fishing and hunting. They make pottery and weave. They live in fenced-in villages of small beehive-shaped houses around a square containing either a large house for bachelors, or the chief's residence. Chiefs and other senior men display their importance by having many wives.

CHIRIGUANO *Population:* unknown. Language group: Tupi-Guarani. Living in the tropical forests of Bolivia, these tribes are the descendants of Guarani who raided the Inca Empire after the Portuguese had conquered their own lands in Brazil. They grow sweet potatoes, maize, pumpkins, tobacco and cotton, and hunt and fish. Men clear and fence fields in the forest. Women weave, make pottery and help in the harvesting. Villages consist of a few large communal houses occupied by people descended from a common male ancestor, and built around a central plaza. When

135

he marries, the man must work for his father-in-law and live with him for a while. There is a hierarchy of male hereditary chiefs from local headmen up to the paramount chief. Only chiefs may have more than one wife.

CHOLON (see LAMA)

CHOROTI (or ZOLATA) *Population:* 2,500. Language group: Matacoan. The Choroti live in Paraguay on the Chaco, mostly by hunting, gathering and fishing, but also by growing a little maize and manioc. Before the Spanish Conquest only dogs were domesticated, but now they also keep horses, sheep, goats and cattle. Villages consist of several houses grouped around a plaza and made of poles and covered with palm leaves and grass. No man may marry a cousin or a local girl, or have more than one wife. A married man helps his wife's parents and often lives with them. Villages have a headman. Over a collection of villages there is a chief, but he lacks real power. On death all personal belongings are destroyed.

COFAN (or QUIJO) *Population:* unknown. Language group: probably Chibchan. The Cofan tribes, about whom little is known, live in the north-east of Ecuador. They cultivate maize, manioc and potatoes and live in villages of mud-plastered houses. They work gold, weave blankets and trade extensively with other tribes. Chiefs often have more than one wife, and pay for her with goods.

COMECHINGON *Population:* unknown. Language group: Comechingon. They live in the heart of Argentina, where they grow maize, beans and quinoa. They farm – sometimes irrigating their fields – keep herds of llamas, and hunt and gather. Their villages, built of half-submerged houses, are led by headmen.

COROA (see Northern CAYAPO)

COROADA (see PURI)

CUBEO *Population:* 2,000. Language group: Tucano. Part of the Tucano (q.v.) family of tribes, the Cubeo live in about 30 groups along the Caiari-Vaupes river. They grow bitter manioc as a staple on slash-and-burn plots. They gather wild foods, and hunt with traps as well as with arrows. They do not inherit land, but fishing rights are closely guarded. They keep pets and live in communal houses, each with an attic for storage, under a headman. The Cubeo, especially their shamans, enjoy smoking huge cigars, and drink their dead relatives' charred remains ground into a soup. They believe in a miraculous infant ancestor, and they are encouraged from childhood to be fierce.

CULINE (see YAMAMADI)

CUMANA *Population:* unknown. Language group: Carib. Along the north-east coast of Venezuela, the numerous Cumana tribes live mostly on bitter manioc, maize and various fruits from trees. The men clear the land for cultivation; women do all the harvesting. They weave and make basket-work and pottery. A few tribes keep ducks. They trade in many goods among their own tribes, and with other tribes for gold. Their villages, of houses with thatched roofs that reach to the ground, are surrounded by several palisades. Only chiefs have more than one wife, and after marriage a man works for his wife's family for one year. Social classes range from slaves to powerful paramount chiefs who are carried on litters.

DESANA (see TUCANO)

DIAGUITA *Population:* unknown. Language group: Diaguitan. The Diaguita are farmers and llama herdsmen who live in middle Chile. They are also talented crafts-men who work copper, gold, silver and bronze, and weave and make pottery. The stone houses of their villages are surrounded by walls and have mud or leaf roofs. A man

may have more than one wife. Headmen are are succeeded by their sons.

DIORE (see Northern CAYAPO)

ENCABELLADO *Population:* unknown. Language group: Tucanoan. Living on the borders of Ecuador, Colombia and Peru, the Encabellado cultivate maize, manioc and sweet potatoes, and hunt and fish. Women do most of the agriculture, except for clearing land. Villages are ruled by headmen who are the only people who may have more than one wife. Once they lived in one-family houses, but now they live mainly in communal long-houses.

GADUVEO (see MBAYA)

GAJARJARA (see TENETEHARA)

GUACHI *Population:* unknown. Language group: Guaicuran. The Guachi live in the western Mato Grosso of Brazil. The rivers play the most important part in the people's lives, but they do grow maize, tobacco and gourds. Blanket weaving is their best-known craft.

GUAHIVO (or GUAHIBO) *Population:* several thousand. Language group: Guahiban. This pre-agricultural tribe lives in the mountainous savanna region of the Vinchada in Colombia – by the headwaters of the Orinoco and Negro rivers. They are nomads led by chiefs and live mainly by hunting and gathering. They weave baskets, make flutes and rattles, and take large quantitites of snuff. Their huts are covered with mats. In the past their large numbers enabled them to wage war on the Achagua (q.v.) and to trade in slaves.

GUAITACA (or WAITACA) *Population:* unknown. Language group: probably Guaitacan. Little is known about them except that they live along the north-east coast of Brazil. They live by hunting and gathering and by growing maize and tubers.

GUAJA *Population:* 100–250. Language group: Tupi-Guarani. The rarely contacted Guaja practise no agriculture, but live in nomadic bands in temporary shelters in the babassu palm tree area near the Gurupi and Upper Pindare rivers, in the state of Maranhao, Brazil.

GUAMO *Population:* unknown. Language group: as yet uncertain. The Guamo are a number of tribes who live in the west part of Venezuela. The majority have no agriculture. Only the Guaicari tribe, once conquered by the Caquetio (q.v.), live in settled villages; the other tribes split into wandering bands and live in temporary camps. Their staple foods are fish and shellfish. They gather honey and fruits, and hunt crocodiles and other animals. In the dry season most Guamo sleep in the open or in palm-leaf shelters. During the rains, some tribes make wickerwork huts in the trees. Men may marry several sisters.

GUANA *Population:* 5,000–5,500. Language group: Arawak. Although the Guana once included many tribes, but are now reduced to the Terena alone, they are still the largest Indian group in the southern Mato Grosso of Brazil. They grow maize and other crops, and hunt and fish. They make pottery, cloth and baskets. Some live in scattered groups, but many live in beehive-shaped huts in large villages of over 1,000 inhabitants, divided into two sections based on kinship. Their society is divided into social classes. In war the villages are led by a chief. Recently the Guana have had much contact with mission-stations and groups of non-Indians.

GUARANI *Population:* 3,000–4,000. Language group: Tupi-Guarani. Most of the numerous Guarani tribes live in the states of Mato Grosso, Parana and north-western Rio Grande do Sul, in Brazil. Most of the people have moved to mission posts. Their villages are large, and the houses hold up to sixty families. Each village is strongly defended and surrounded by several palisades as well as by a series of moats. Maize is their staple. They also fish and hunt, and gather pine nuts and palm fruits. Only headmen and shamans may have more than one wife, and marriage with a first cousin is preferred. They do not work metals

themselves, but they trade over long distances, or raid other settlements for gold and silver ornaments.
(pages 106-111)

GUARAYU *Population:* unknown. Language group: Tupi-Guarani. The two little-known tribes that make up the Guarayu live along the Brazilian border in Bolivia, hunting, fishing and cultivating their staples of maize and manioc. They also weave, and make bark cloth and crude pottery. Several families live together in one house. Men can marry more than one wife. Before marriage, preferably to a first cousin, a man must live with his bride's father and give him a number of presents.

GUAYAKI *Population:* unknown. Language group: Tupi-Guarani. They live in wandering bands in the extreme south of Paraguay and in east Argentina near the Brazilian border. In bands of about 20 people led by a headman they hunt, and gather honey, various parts of the pindo palm and beetle larvae. They make baskets, weave nettle fibers, and live in huts made of poles and palm leaves. When a man marries he lives with his wife's band. Only a headman may have more than one wife.

GUAYUPE *Population:* unknown. Language group: Arawak. The Guayupe live in the heart of Colombia, where they fish and grow maize, peanuts, peppers and manioc. Each of their houses in the fenced-in villages has room for several families. Marriages are made within the village. Before he marries the man gives presents to his bride's father. He can have more than one wife.

ITONAMA *Population:* unknown. Language group: Itonaman. This little-known tribe lives in large villages in north-east Bolivia close to the Brazilian border. They cultivate, hunt and fish.

IPURINAN *Population:* 500–1,000. Language group: Arawak. They live in the Brazilian state of Amazonas near the Acre, Seruini and Ituxi rivers, fishing from bark canoes, hunting, and growing maize, cotton

and manioc. Their villages are small merely a couple of huts with thatched roofs that reach down to the ground, occupied by half a dozen families

JIVARO *Population:* 20,000. Language group: Jivaran. Famous as headhunters the Jivaro live in south Ecuador and Peru. They hunt game and are agriculturalists who keep llamas and pigs and turn their sweet manioc into beer which they drink in great quantities. Their villages consist of a single house occupied by many relatives. In time of war, related households unite under a temporary chief; otherwise matters are decided by the head of the household. Women outnumber men by about two to one, because Jivaro bands are constantly at war with one another, and capture and shrink the heads of their victims. If a household is attacked, all except young women, who willingly give themselves up, are killed. So houses are well-hidden, with many defences: for example, the nearby paths are often booby-trapped. They bury their dead under the house floor, but corpses of more important people are suspended from the ceiling and their houses abandoned.
(pages 38-41)

JURI (see MANAO)

JURUNA A tribe that now lives in the Xingu National Park (q.v.).

KALAPALO A tribe of Carib origin that now lives in the Xingu National Park (q.v.).

KAMAYURA A tribe of Tupi origin that now lives in the Xingu National Park (q.v.).

KAYABI A tribe that now lives inside the Xingu National Park (q.v.).

KITEMOCA *Population:* unknown. Language group: Chapacuran. Nothing is known about this tribe except that it lives in Amazonia, in the east of Bolivia.

KREEN-AKRORE *Population:* several hundred. Language group: unknown. Called 'people of the short hair' by their neighbors, the Kreen-Akrore live in the central Brazilian wilderness. They were unknown until the 1960s and, at the time of writing, had only been seen by outsiders from an airplane. They live in large huts roofed with banana leaves, and sleep closely packed on the floors of their wall-less houses. They do not use the slash-and-burn techniques of their neighbors, but grow bananas and corn in elaborate geometrically pattered gardens. They use large clubs and stone axes whose size suggests that the Kreen-Akrore are huge people, probably seven feet tall. They are probably unable to swim or use canoes, and are sorely threatened by the approach of the Trans-Amazon Highway.
(pages 54-55)

KUIKURO A tribe of Carib origin that now lives in the Xingu National Park (q.v.).

LAMA *Population:* unknown. Language group: Laman. The Lama tribes, including the Cholon, live in Peru near the Huallaga and Maronon rivers. People, usually related through males, live together in villages. They grow sweet manioc, maize, peanuts and cotton, hunt, fish, weave and make pottery.

LENGUA (see MASCOI)

LOCONO (see ARAWAK)

MACA *Population:* unknown. Language group: probably Matacoan. The little-known Maca tribes live in south Paraguay to the west of Asunción, hunting, growing crops and making pottery.

MACU (or BOROWA) *Population:* unknown. Language group: Macu. The seldom-contacted, little-known nomadic Macu live in the north-west Amazonas of Brazil. They hunt, fish, grow crops and live in temporary shelters made of branches and leaves. Neighboring tribes (for example the Cubeo q.v.) fear them for their sorcery.

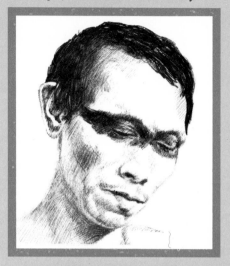

MACURAP *Population:* 50. Language group: Tupi-Guarani. The Macurap, including the Arua, live along the tributaries of the Guapore river in the state of Rondonia, Brazil. They grow maize and other crops and keep dogs and ducks. Their beehive-shaped houses, built around a central pole. are divided into compartments for each family.

MACUSI *Population:* 2,000–3,000. Language group: Carib. The Macusi live in the Brazilian territory of Rio Branco where they grow bitter manioc, hunt, fish and trade with other tribes. Women tend the crops; men help plant and harvest. Their houses, made of bark, palm or thatch, vary in shape and size. Men have only one wife, preferably a first cousin, and live with their wife's parents.

MAKRITARE (or YECUANA) *Population:* several hundred. Language group: Carib. The Makritare live in large communal houses on the Merevari, Paraoa and upper Mazanimi rivers of Guyana, where they grow bitter manioc on shifting plots, kill fish with poison and animals with blowguns. They take a narcotic called banisteriopsis, and hold carved wooden replicas of animals when they dance. They weave the hair of slain enemies into their belts.

MANAO *Population:* unknown. Language group: Arawak. The Manao tribes, among whom the best-known are the Juri and the Pase (possibly extinct) live in Brazil's Amazonas. They grow maize and manioc as staples, keep slaves and live in circular houses. Chiefs may control more than one village, and only they are likely to have more than one wife. The Manao make unusually large canoes.

MASCO *Population:* unknown. Language group: Arawak. This little-known group of Peruvian tribes lives in communal houses in small villages near Brazil's south-eastern border. They grow sweet manioc and hunt and fish.

MASCOI *Population:* 2,300. Language group Mascoian. The semi-nomadic Mascoi group of tribes, the best-known of which is the Lengua, lives in central Paraguay. They live in small bands under hereditary head-men. They grow a few crops and keep increasing numbers of cattle, sheep and horses and also hunt, fish and gather. They sleep in temporary shelters made of poles, reed mats, or of branches and leaves. Newly-married men at first live with their parents-in-law and generally have but one wife.

MASHACALI *Population:* 100–250. Language group: Mashacali. They live near the headwaters of the Itanhaem river in Brazil's Minas Gerais, and are in permanent contact with mission stations. They add to their diet of maize and beans by hunting and gathering, but rarely fish. Their dome-shaped houses are each occupied by one family. A man may marry several sisters.

MATACO *Population:* 20,000. Language group: Matacoan. The Mataco live in north-east Argentina as semi-nomads, moving from one settlement to another in bands led by headmen and named after animals, objects and parts of the body. They fish a lot, and herd horses, sheep and goats, but do not rely on agriculture. A married couple spend the first months of marriage with the girl's parents, and then set up their own home.

MATAPUHY A tribe of Carib origin that now lives in the Xingu National Park (q.v.).

MAUE *Population:* 1,400. Language group: Tupi-Guarani. The Maue, most of whom are integrated with other tribes, live in settled villages of thatched huts, one for each family, in the Brazilian state of Amazonas. They grow manioc as their staple, and hunt, gather, and fish. They have both bark and dugout canoes. Their hereditary chiefs are powerful. All men may have more than one wife.

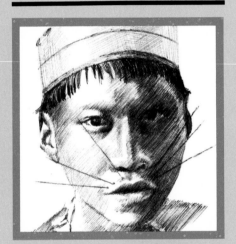

MAYORUNA (or MAYA) *Population:* 200–500. Language group: Panoan. The Mayoruna live in villages along the frontiers of the Peruvian and Brazilian Amazonas. They hunt, fish and gather, and they grow sweet manioc and maize. Men may have more than one wife. The Mayoruna are warlike and have in the past forced settlers to withdraw from their area.

MBAYA *Population:* 100–250. Language group: Guaicuran. The Mbaya, whose largest tribe is the Gaduveo, live on the borders of Paraguay and Brazil, hunting and fishing for their main diet. From the Spanish they adopted horses for their raids on other tribes. Their temporary houses are made of mats laid over poles. They have a complicated class structure with various hereditary chiefs and other nobles, who alone may have more than one wife. After marriage, enacted by exchanges of presents, the man lives with his bride's family.

MEHINAKU A tribe of Arawak origin that now lives in the Xingu National Park (q.v.).

MENTUKTIRE (see Northern CAYAPO)

MOCOVI *Population:* unknown. Language group: Guiacuran. The Mocovi are nomadic hunters who live in northern Argentina camping in rough shelters and eating locusts as their main food. They adopted cattle and horses from the Spaniards. The young men must undergo many rituals to gain admittance into the warrior class. Men usually have only one wife.

MOJO *Population:* small. Language group: Arawak. The Mojo are now fully integrated with other local tribes, and have adopted much from European culture. Their past indigenous culture, based on agriculture, hunting and fishing was rich. Their society was divided into social classes and they practised a jaguar-hunting and spirit cult which entailed the use of large drinking houses. They built large canals and bridges.

MUNDURUCU *Population:* 1,000–1,500. Language group: Tupi-Guarani. Most of the Mundurucu, who live along the Tapajos river of Brazil, are still hostile, and were wellknown as head-hunters. They are skilled in feather-work. They grow, hunt and gather food and live in settled villages with a men's house. They have distinct social classes and chiefs for war and peace, who may have a second wife who is often a captive. Some Mundurucu have settled as rubber collectors near mission stations.

MURA *Population:* 1,000–1,500. Language group: Mura. They live in small villages of thatched houses along the banks of the Autaz, Madeira and neighboring rivers and tributaries in the Brazilian state of Amazonas. They often settle around mission stations. Fishing, from well-made bark canoes, is their chief source of food, although they also grow manioc and maize. Marriage sometimes entails working for the girl's parents. At times in their history

the Mura men have been allowed several wives. Each village has a hereditary headman.

NAMBICUARA *Population:* 500–1,000. Language group: Nambicuara. Living in the north-western Mato Grosso near the Aripuana river, some of the Nambicuara tribes have settled near the mission and Indian stations, but most are only occasionally contacted. During the rains they build temporary villages and grow sweet and bitter manioc, maize and other crops. In the dry season they split into small bands and live by hunting, fishing and gathering, and sleep in temporary shelters. At marriage, preferably with a first cousin, they exchange presents. Leaders sometimes have more than one wife.

NAHUKWA A tribe of Carib origin that now lives in the Xingu National Park (q.v.).

NAPO (see CANELO)

OMAGUA *Population:* unknown. Language group: unknown. The Omagua live in northernmost Argentina. They keep llamas for their wool, and grow maize and quinoa. They sometimes use terraced irrigation, and work copper and bronze. Their villages, which they sometimes fortify, are of several stone huts with flat reed and mud roofs. Chiefs rule several villages.

OTOMAC *Population:* unknown. Language group: Otomacan. The Otomac live in south Venezuela on the fertile flood plain of the Orinoco river in villages, which are independent collections of shelters lining the river banks. They fish, and catch turtles, crocodiles and manatees. They grow maize and women take no part in their agriculture. There are no chiefs, but some villages have councils. Most men have several wives.

OTUKE *Population:* unknown. Language group: Otukean. The Otuke live in Bolivia

139

near the Chiquito tribe (q.v.) with whom they have largely integrated. Little is known about their original culture.

OUYANA, OYANA (see TRIO)

PACAGUARA *Population:* unknown. Language group: Panoan. The few survivors of these tribes live in north-east Bolivia and western Brazil growing sweet manioc and maize as staple foods. Their rectangular, gabled houses each accommodate one family. Every village has a special house for men.

PALIKUR *Population:* 500–700. Language group: Arawak. Of the two main surviving groups of Palikur the largest lives in Brazil near the town of Oiapoque near the Urucaua river. The other group lives across the French Guiana border. Most of the Palikur are fully integrated into the Brazilian way of life. Those still in the bush live in circular houses built on piles and grow manioc and catch fish from dug-out canoes, noted for their excellence. Villages elect a headman. Men are allowed only one wife and live with their bride's parents until they can clear their own land and build a house.

PARAKOTO (see WAIWAI)

PARESSI *Population:* 250. Language group: Arawak. The surviving Paressi live in small

settlements near the headwaters of the Juruena river in Brazil. Although they trade with local settlers, they largely keep to themselves. They grow maize, manioc, beans and cotton, and keep bees and hunting dogs. They do not use canoes. They build roads and pathways between their small settlements of a ceremonial house and one or two oval-shaped houses, each holding six families. They have hereditary headmen, but chiefs are rare and arise through conquest. A man usually marries several sisters.

PASE (see MANAO)

PAUMARI *Population:* 250–500. Language group: Arawak. The Paumari live in permanent settlements on the islands and sandbanks of the River Purus, in the Brazilian state of Amazonas. Most are in constant contact with local white Brazilians. They hunt, gather, grow maize and obtain their main diet of fish and turtles from finely made canoes. In the flood season they live on raft-houses on the rivers, in the dry season in small land-huts covered with palm-mats.

PAYAGUA *Population:* unknown. Language group: Guaicuran. Now fully integrated into South America's western way of life. The Payagua used to live along the upper reaches of the River Paraguay, where they were known as South America's finest river men: the Spaniards called them 'the river pirates'. Their largest dugout canoes carried over 40 men. Wild rice was their staple, but they also ate a lot of fish. Chiefs had pierced lips and were carried on litters.

PILAGA *Population:* unknown. Language group: Guaicuran. The Pilaga live in the region of the Gran Chaco in Argentina and Paraguay where they hunt, fish, gather, and grow a few crops. They have horses and dogs, and live in villages of communal houses grouped around a plaza or along a central street. Men marry girls from outside the immediate locality.

PIRO *Population:* unknown. Language group: Arawak. The little-known Piro live

in eastern Peru. They hunt, fish, grow crops, weave and make bark cloth. They live in independent settlements in which each family has its own circular or rectangular thatched house. A man may marry several wives, and must work for his bride's father.

PUELCHE *Population:* unknown. Language group: Puelche. The Puelche live in the Argentinian pampas south of the River Plate. They adopted horses from the Spanish, but for a long time kept their language and customs. Although they still hunt a great deal, education and travel have tuned them into peasant farmers who live in houses on farms and grow crops introduced by Europeans.

PUINAVE *Population:* unknown. Language group: Puinavean. The little-known Puinave live in eastern Colombia to the west of the Venezuelan border. They practise a little agriculture, but live mostly by hunting, fishing and gathering. Their huts are temporary, and shaped like pyramids with leaves and branches to cover them.

PURI *Population:* unknown. Language group: Puri-Coroado. Neither fishing nor agriculture are of much importance to this collection of tribes who live mostly in the Minas Gerais state of eastern Brazil. They are nomadic hunters and gatherers who wander around in small bands led by the oldest man. At night they shelter in simple palm-branch lean-to huts. The Coroada tribe build gabled huts with thatched roofs reaching to the ground. Only a few men have more than one wife.

QUIJO (see COFAN)

SALIVA *Population:* unknown. Language group: Salivan. Probably extinct, the Saliva lived in the plains of Colombia near the Orinoco river fishing and growing maize and sweet manioc. Their villages were led by headmen, but they had no real power.

SARAVECA *Population:* unknown.

Language group: Arawak. The Saraveca live in Bolivia near the Brazilian border and are almost completely integrated with the Chiquito (q.v.).

SHAVANTE *Population:* 2,500–3,000. Language group: Ge. Since being contacted in 1954, the Shavante, who live near the Rio das Mortes and the Xingu river in Brazil, have gradually ceased to be nomadic. They now farm increasingly, living in independent horseshoe-shaped villages on the open savanna. Although they have a passion for meat, they live primarily off roots, nuts and fruits. They are divided into clans. A man must marry from outside his clan, and is likely to have several wives, especially if he is a chief. (q.v. Caraja, Sherente).

SHERENTE *Population:* 250–500. Language group: Ge. The Sherente live east of the Tocantis river in Brazil where they grow manioc and maize, and gather, hunt and fish. Their villages consist of single-family houses, in a horseshoe pattern around a bachelors' hut. They are similar to, and may once have been the same people as, the Shavante (q.v.) but have had comparatively more contact with mission stations. Sherente can now speak Portuguese.

SHIRIANA (see YANOMAMO)

SIRIONO *Population:* 2,000–3,000. Language group: Tupi-Guarani. This east Bolivian tribe is made up of nomadic bands, each about 50 strong, led by not very powerful headmen. They are famous for their effective longbow, and their 8-10 feet long arrows. They hunt, gather and fish, grow a little sweet manioc and maize, and live in temporary shelters of poles lashed to trees and covered with palm leaves. The preferred marriage is with the mother's brother's daughter. Unlike nearby tribes, they have shamans. They believe that the spirit of the moon gave them their culture. During the last few years they retreated deeper into the jungle, to avoid contact with settlers.

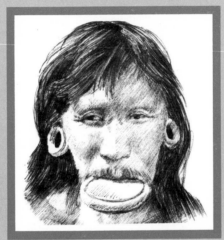

SUYA *Population:* about 70. Language group: Ge. The Suya live east of the headwaters of Brazil's Rio Culuene, a source of the Xingu river. Although once numerically strong, they have been rapidly dying out since contact with the white man. They now live inside the Xingu National Park (q.v.). They grow manioc and maize and hunt and fish; they live in independent villages of a few long communal houses with thatched roofs that reach to the ground.

TACANA *Population:* unknown. Language group: Tacanan. The numerous Tacana tribes live in eastern Bolivia and Brazil's western Mato Grosso, where they grow sweet manioc, maize and peppers as staples and gather Brazil nuts and fruits from the forest. Their villages consist of a few families living in one hut, led by a hereditary headman who alone is allowed more than one wife.

TAPIETE *Population:* unknown. Language group: Tupi-Guarani. This group lives mostly in large semi-nomadic hunting bands in Paraguay near the Bolivian border. Although they speak a Tupi-Guarani language, their origins are probably Matacoan (q.v.).

TAPIRAPE *Population:* 50. Language group: Tupi-Guarani. This tiny Tupi tribe of the eastern Mato Grosso now lives in a village at an Indian post. Formerly they depended on agriculture, supplemented by some hunting and fishing, mainly for turtles and their eggs. Men cultivated manioc, maize, beans and pumpkins, while women cultivated peanuts and cotton. Their main crafts are pottery and basketry. Their houses are rectangular and arranged in an oval pattern. Each settlement once had special feasting groups, and men were allowed only one wife.

TAULIPANG *Population:* 1,000–1,500. Language group: Carib. The Taulipang are a warlike people who live on the borders of Brazil, Venezuela and Guyana, particularly in the mountainous territory of Brazil's Rio Branco. They grow bitter manioc and maize, and gather lizard eggs, honey and insect larvae. Their canoes are made of bark. Their villages, which are led by hereditary headmen, consist of several round houses sometimes built on piles. A man, who may marry several wives, works for the bride-to-be's father and on marriage goes to live within his house.

TEMBE (see TENETEHARA)

TENETEHARA *Population:* 3,000. Language group: Tupi-Guarani. The main Tenetehara tribes, the Tembe, Gajarjara, and the lesser Urubuj-Kaapor, live on the eastern edge of the Amazon forest in Brazil. Most have settled near Indian posts and now keep animals. They grow peanuts and cotton and, as their staples, maize and manioc. Their village houses are built of poles and palm leaves and line a long central street. Most men have a single wife, except household heads who often have several.

141

TEREMEMBE *Population:* unknown. Language group: possibly Ge. This little-known tribe lives on the north-east coast of Brazil, mostly by fishing and hunting in small, nomadic bands.

TERENA (see GUANA)

TICUNA (see TUCUNA)

TIMBIRA *Population:* 2,000–3,000. Language group: Ge. Over half the Timbira tribes are now extinct, since contact with Brazilian settlers. The best known survivors are the Canella in Maranhao and the Craho in North Goias, (who are both in permanent contact with Brazilians) and the Gavioes, who are the most numerous and isolated and live in south-east Para. They all grow manioc, sweet potatoes and maize as their chief crops and live in thatched houses. Villages are divided into two main kinship groups ruled by headmen with the help of a council of elders.

TOBA *Population:* 10,000. Language group: Guaicuran. The Toba of north-east Argentina live in migratory bands mainly by fishing, but also hunt and cultivate maize, pumpkins, manioc and tobacco. While the men hunt, the women help with the farming and make pottery. The Toba keep dogs, sheep, goats and horses. Their bands, which are organized under a headman and a council of elders, were originally named after animals, natural objects, and parts of the body. Most men have only one wife and at marriage the bridegroom gives presents of fish and game to the bride's parents.

TONOCOTE *Population:* unknown. Language group: unknown. Now either extinct or absorbed into another people the Tonocote once lived in north central Argentine, where they grew maize, beans, quinoa and squash, hunted and fished, and kept llamas, turkey and rhea (an ostrich-like bird). Their main crafts were pottery, weaving woolen fabrics and copper-work.

Their villages consisted of clusters of grass huts.

TRIO (or WAIYANA, OUYANA, OYANA) *Population:* 800. Language group: Carib. Most of this tribe have now settled at mission stations on the Brazilian and Guyana borders. They eat manioc as a staple food and hunt, fish, and collect Brazil nuts and honey. They paint geometrical designs on their bodies. Their villages are led by headmen. A man may marry several sisters. Adultery is common.

TRUMAI *Population:* 50. Language group: Trumai. Only one Trumai group survives, in the Xingu National Park (q.v.) at the source of the Rio Xingu in the Mato Grosso of Brazil. They grow manioc, peppers and beans and trade extensively with other tribes. They live, several families to a large house, in villages on river banks. Cousins are forbidden to marry.

TUCANO *Population:* 3,000–4,000. Language group: Tucano. The Tucano, who include the Cubeo (q.v.), Barasana (q.v.) and several other related tribes, have had much recent contact with rubber plantations and the manioc trades. They grow most of their food, but also hunt and fish. Men may only marry girls from other villages, often

by the exchange of sisters. Villages may consist of a single house that holds many families, are normally independent, and are led by a headman.

TUCUNA (or TICUNA) *Population:* 1,000–1,500. Language group: Tucuna. In Peru and Brazil, near the Ica and Salimoes rivers, the Tucuna are now in permanent contact with Indian stations. They fish, and grow maize and manioc. Their straw-walled houses, sometimes raised on piles, hold several families. Women are not allowed to live far from their parents, so sons-in-law come to live near the bride's family.

TUPI *Population:* unknown. Language group: Tupi-Guarani. The Tupi of the Rio São Francisco live in the interior of east Brazil. They are less well-known than the Tupinamba (q.v.), their coastal relatives, who live in settled agricultural villages.

TUPINAMBA *Population:* 10,000. Language group: Tupi-Guarani. The Tupinamba live on the Atlantic sea-coast of Brazil from São Paulo north to the Amazon river, and have largely lost their tribal culture and language. Formerly they were a violent people, living in stockaded hilltop villages where they kept slaves destined to be cannibalistically eaten. Many men had several wives, each with her own private apartment. They grew manioc, maize, beans, pumpkins, sweet potatoes, peanuts and tobacco, and hunted and gathered wild fruits and nuts. As they lived near the sea, fish yielded the bulk of their food at certain seasons. Each village had a headman and a council of elders and warriors.

TXICAO A tribe that recently attacked the Yaruma (q.v.) and now lives in the Xingu National Park (q.v.).

TXUKAHAMAI A tribe that now lives in the Xingu National Park (q.v.). The men wear hip-discs. The tribe's survival is gravely threatened by the planned highway through its land.

URUBUJ-KAAPOR (see TENETEHARA)

VILELA *Population:* unknown. Language group: Lule-Vilelan. The little-known Vilela live in north Argentina, some live peacefully, growing crops in settled villages, while others lead a war-like, nomadic life.

WAIKA (see YANOMAMO)

WAITACA (see GUAITACA)

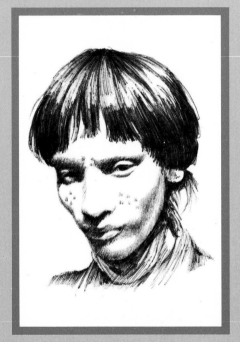

WAIWAI *Population:* 1,000. Language group: Carib. The Waiwai include many similar tribes, especially the Parakoto. They live in villages of one round communal house which are moved to a new site every five years so that on new land they can grow bitter manioc, sugar cane and (since Europeans came) bananas. They also hunt and fish. The Waiwai are well-known for their longbows and for their musical instruments and they trade with other tribes for arrow reeds and ornaments. Their villages are ruled by a village chief. There are several age grades for both sexes. Men often marry several sisters. All deaths, except those of the very young and the very old, are believed to be by sorcery; a revenge party is likely to attack the village of the suspected culprit.

WAIYANA (see TRIO)

WANANA (see TUCANO)

WAPISHANA *Population:* 4,000. Language group: Arawak. The Wapishana of south-west Guyana have almost wholly lost their traditional way of life; even the once isolated Maopityan (q.v.) now live with the Waiwai (q.v.). They live mainly by growing crops, including their staple, manioc, and by fishing, hunting and gathering. Men hunt and trade, women cultivate the fields and make pottery. The village huts each contain several families.

WARRAU *Population:* 7,000–8,000. Language group: Warrau. This is a single tribe of hunters and gatherers living in the Orinoco delta where they were probably recently forced to move. Although they grow plantations, sugar cane, watermelons, peppers and manioc, their staple diet is the pith of the Mauritia palm-tree. The men fish, trade with other tribes and make baskets; the women make pottery and tend the crops. The Warrau live in thatched, rectangular houses that hold several families. Each village has a headman.

WAURU (or WAUSHA) *Population:* 100–150. Language group: Arawak. They live near the Batovi source of Brazil's Rio Xingu where they are gradually increasing their contacts with nearby Indian posts. They trade extensively, and grow many crops, chifly manioc and maize. They also fish from bark canoes, hunt and gather. Their villages are independent and consist of a few thatched oval houses each occupied by several families.

WAYANA (see TRIO)

WITOTO *Population:* several thousand. Language group: Witotan. The Witoto live in south Colombia and extend into Brazil and Peru where they grow manioc, maize and tobacco. Men hunt, fish and gather, women tend the crops and make pottery. The entire community of a village lives in one large hut presided over by a village council. The headman of the council is the only man who may have more than one wife.

XIKRIN A tribe of the Northern Cayapo (q.v.).

Glossary

(pages 22-31)

XINGU This is not the name of a tribe but of one of the Amazon river's largest tributaries. It runs through the Xingu National Park, a reserve for Indians. It was created in 1961, and at the time of writing, 15 tribes of varying cultures all co-exist inside the Park. They would almost certainly die out but for the Park and its creators, the Villas Boas brothers. The Kamayura and Aweti tribes are of Tupi origin. The Mehinaku, Waura (or Wausha q.v.) and Yawalapiti are of Arawak descent, while the Park's Carib descendants are the Kuikuro, Kalapalo, Matapuhy and Nahukwa peoples. The other tribes in the Park are the Trumai (q.v.), Txicao (q.v.), Txukahamai (q.v.), Suya (q.v.), Kayabi and Juruna.
(pages 42-53)

YAGUA *Population:* 1,000. Language group: Peban. The Yagua live in northern Peru, occasionally fishing and growing crops, but living mostly by hunting. An entire village, lives together in one very large oval hut. Settlements are independent and are ruled by a headman and his council. Each man has one wife and on marriage must work for his father-in-law for a number of years.

YAMAMADI *Population* 500–1,000.

Language group: Arawak. The Culine are the best known tribe of this group that lives between the Jurua and Purus rivers in Brazil and they are now mostly in permanent contact with the nearby Indian posts. The Yamamadi grow their chief diet of sweet manioc, maize and other crops, and hunt, fish from bark canoes, and gather wild fruits and nuts. Their villages, which are independent, are made up of one vast round house as much as 130 feet in diameter with low walls and cone-shaped thatched roof as high as 70 feet.

YANOMAMO (or SHIRIANA or WAIKA) *Population:* 10,000. Language group: unknown. The warlike Yanomamo live in southern Venezuela and across the Brazilian border, and are still relatively isolated. They are sometimes called Shiriana, which in the tongue of their northern neighbors, the Makritare (q.v.), means 'howler monkey'. Some anthropologists call them Waika, from the Yanomamo verb *waikao* which means 'to kill and animal or man that is already dying from a wound'. They hunt wild pig, armadillos, anteaters, tapirs, deer and small birds, collect wild honey, fruit and insects, but mostly eat home-grown plantation. They now clear the land with steel tools. Their settlements are of one large oval communal hut with a conical roof, usually surrounded by their garden plots. The Yanomamo frequently raid each other to capture women and kill men. They cremate corpses and grind their bones to powder, add this to a special soup and drink it.

YARUMA *Population:* 100. Language group: Carib. Ever since the Yaruma, who live along the upper Xingu in the Mato Grosso state of Brazil, were recently attacked by an uncontacted tribe called the Txikao they have come to Indian and mission stations for protection. They fish, grow bitter manioc and maize as their staples, hunt and gather wild fruits. Their villages are made up of a circle of a few large communal houses, with arched thatched roofs that reach down to the ground.

YARURO *Population:* 200–300. Language group: Yaruro. They are an isolated, mobile people who live along the banks of

several tributaries of the Orinoco river. They catch fish from 18 foot dugout canoes and hunt crocodiles, manatees, turtles, deer and armadillos. During the dry season, they are constantly on the move. In the rainy season they settle in semi-permanent villages. Split into little bands, they come together only for ceremonial purposes.

YAWALAPITI A tribe of Arawak descent that lives in the Xingu National Park (q.v.).

YECUANA (see MAKRITARE)

YURUNA *Population:* 300–400. Language group: Tupi-Guarani. The largest surviving tribe of this isolated group, which lives in Brazil's northern Mato Grosso and Para, is the Asurini (q.v.). The Yaruna grow manioc as their staple. Some tribes fish from dugout canoes, while other catch crocodiles. Their small settlements, led by a hereditary headman, are often defensively sited on islands. Men are allowed only a single wife.

ZAMUCO *Population:* unknown. Language group: Zamucoan. The Zamuco live in north Paraguay where they cultivate maize, beans, manioc and peanuts. Men hunt but most of the food is supplied by the women, who gather wild fruits and roots. Some of these people used to keep slaves.

ZAPARO *Population:* small. Language group: Zaparoan. They live in the Montana region on the borders of Ecuador and Peru. They are peaceful farmers who also hunt and fish. The Zaporo may have invented the blowgun, which probably originated in this area.

ZOLATA (see CHOROTI)

All population figures are approximate.